# ACROSS THE UNIVERSE

ISBN: 978-1-4234-3462-7

HAL•LEONARD®
CORPORATION

7777 W. BLUEMOUND RD. P.O. BOX 13819 MILWAUKEE, WI 53213

Visit Hal Leonard Online at
**www.halleonard.com**

# GIRL

Words and Music by JOHN LENNON
and PAUL McCARTNEY

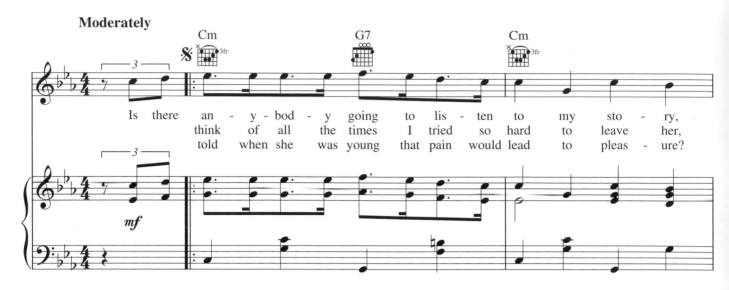

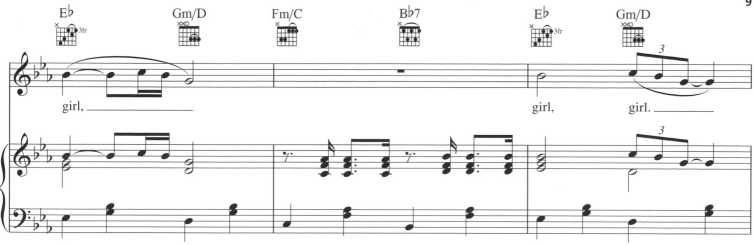

girl, _____ girl, girl. _____

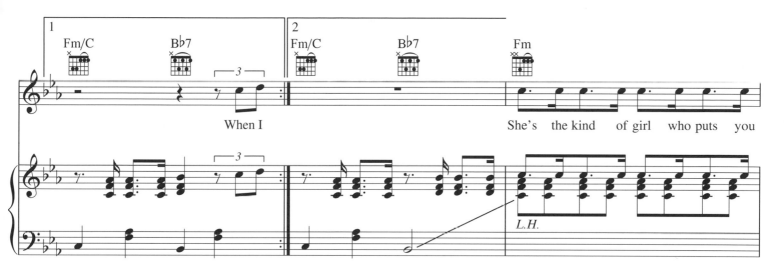

When I

She's the kind of girl who puts you

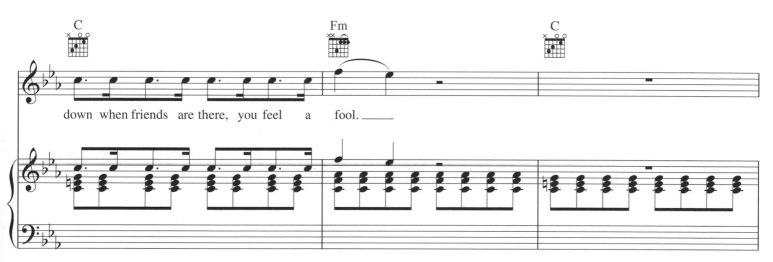

down when friends are there, you feel a fool. _____

When you say she's look - ing good, she acts as if it's un - der - stood. She's

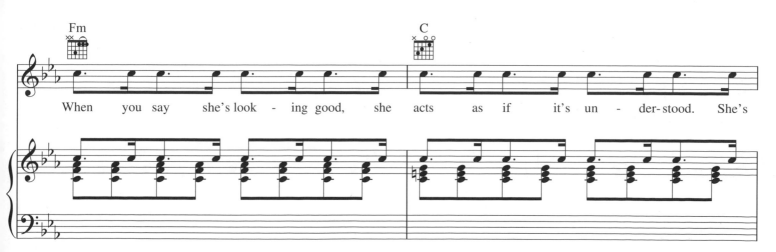

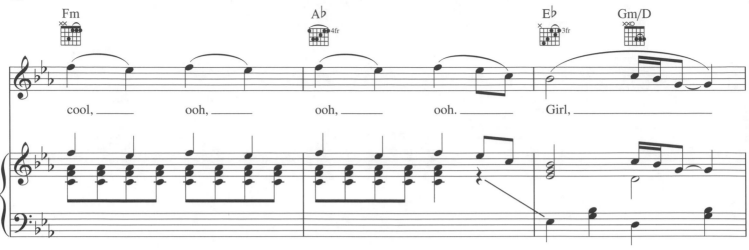

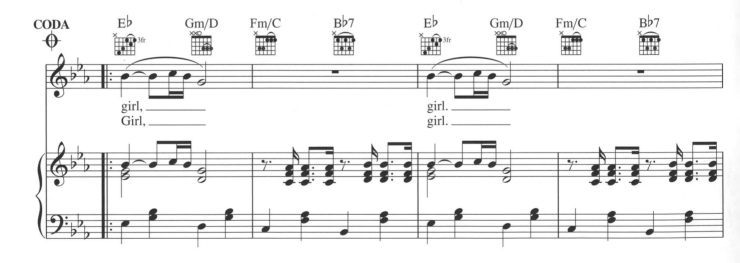

# LET IT BE

Words and Music by JOHN LENNON
and PAUL McCARTNEY

When I find my-self __ in times of trou-ble

*Instrumental*

Moth-er Mar - y comes to me speak-ing words of wis - dom; let it be. __ And in my hour of dark - ness, she is

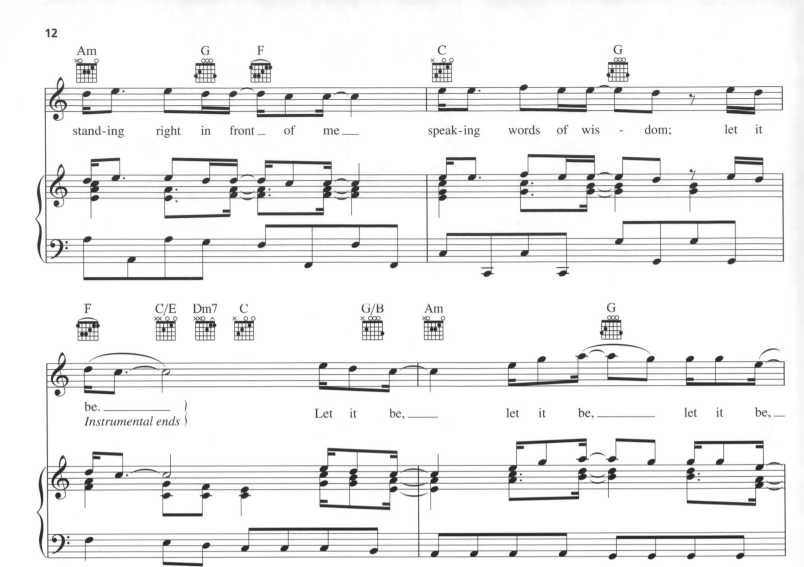

stand-ing right in front _ of me _ speak-ing words of wis - dom; let it

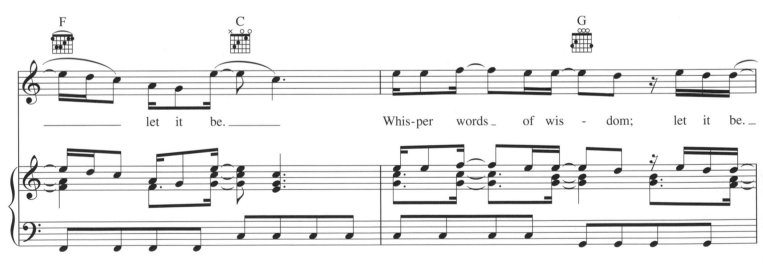

be. _____
*Instrumental ends*

Let it be, _____ let it be, _____ let it be, _

_____ let it be. _____ Whis-per words _ of wis - dom; let it be. _

_____
{ And when __ the bro - ken - heart - ed peo - ple
{ And when __ the night _ is cloud - y, there is

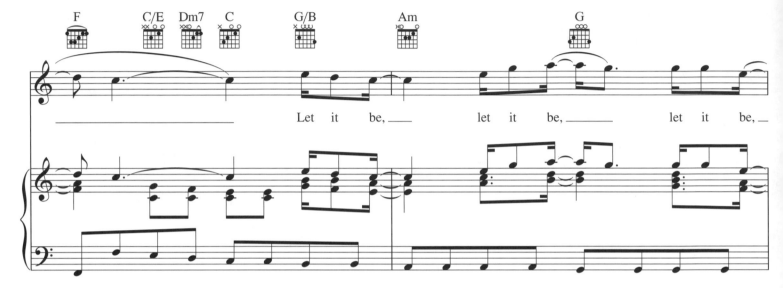

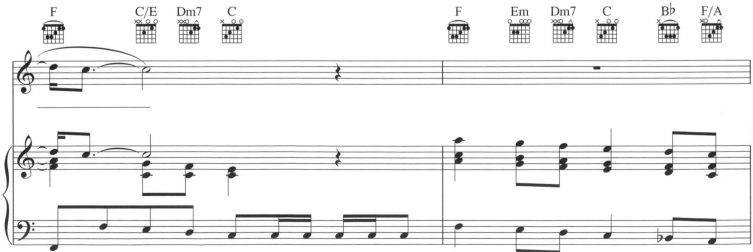

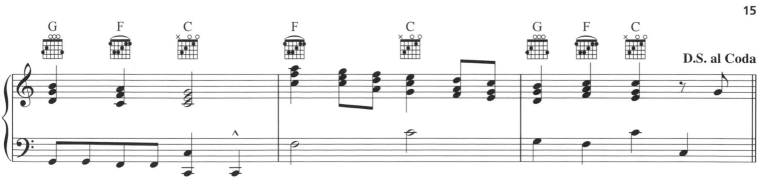

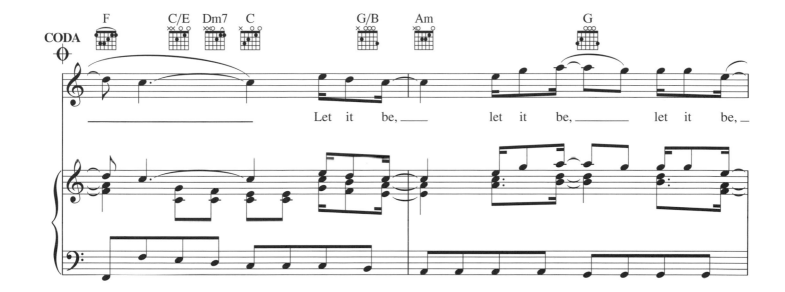

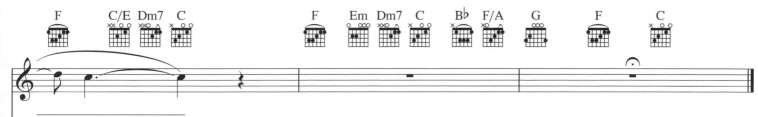

# HOLD ME TIGHT

Words and Music by JOHN LENNON
and PAUL McCARTNEY

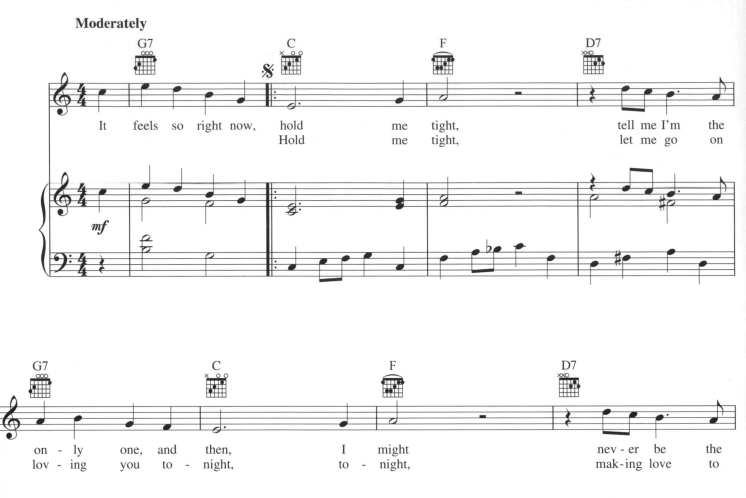

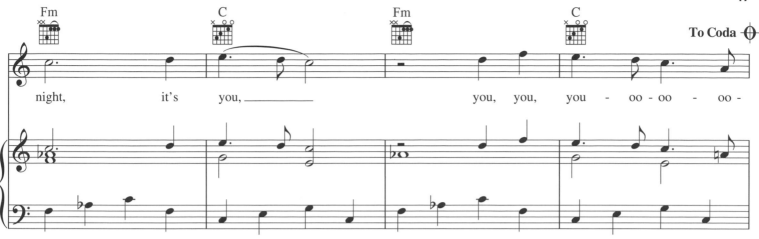

To Coda ⊕

night,　　it's you,　_____　　you,　you,　you - oo - oo - oo -

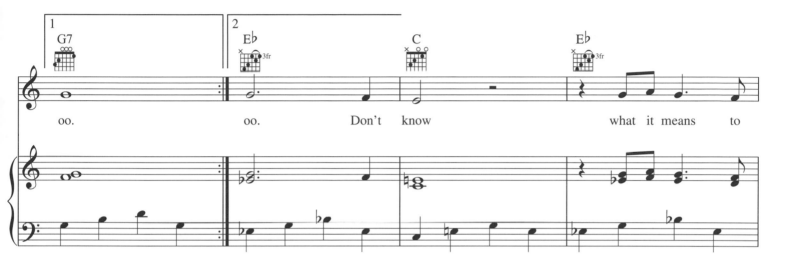

oo.　　　oo.　　Don't know　　what it means to

hold you tight,　　be - ing here a - lone to - night with　you. ____　　It

**D.S. al Coda**
**(Verse 1)**

feels so right now,

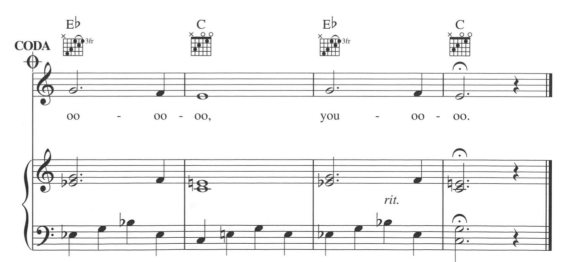

**CODA**

oo - oo - oo,　　you - oo - oo.

*rit.*

# ALL MY LOVING

Words and Music by JOHN LENNON
and PAUL McCARTNEY

**Moderately fast, with a Swing feel**

Close your eyes and I'll kiss _____ you, _____ to-
tend that I'm kiss - ing _____ the

mor - row _____ I'll miss _____ you; _____ re - mem - ber _____ I'll
lips I _____ am miss - ing _____ and hope that _____ my

al - ways _____ be true. _____
dreams will _____ come true. _____

And then

while I'm a - way, ___ I'll write home ev - 'ry day ___

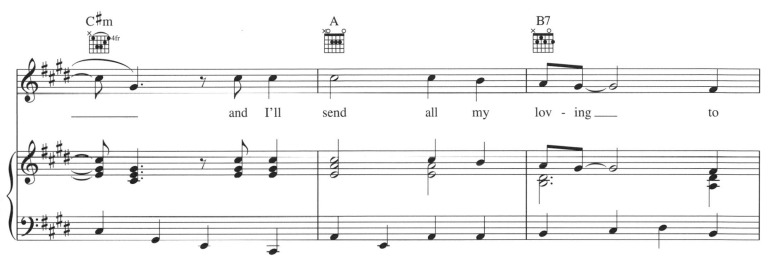

___ and I'll send all my lov - ing ___ to

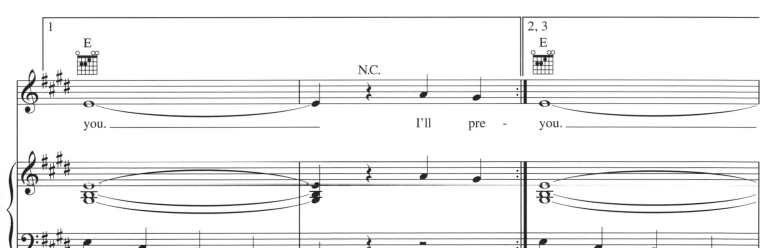

you. ___ I'll pre - you. ___

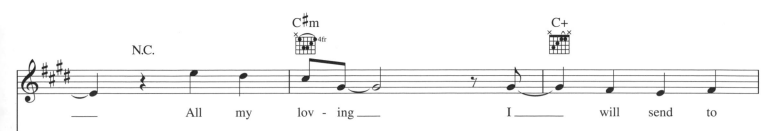

___ All my lov - ing ___ I ___ will send to

you, _____ all \_\_\_ my lov-ing, \_\_\_ dar-

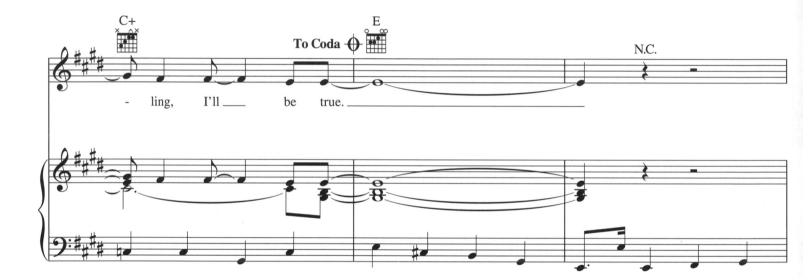

**To Coda**

**N.C.**

-ling, I'll \_\_\_ be true. _____

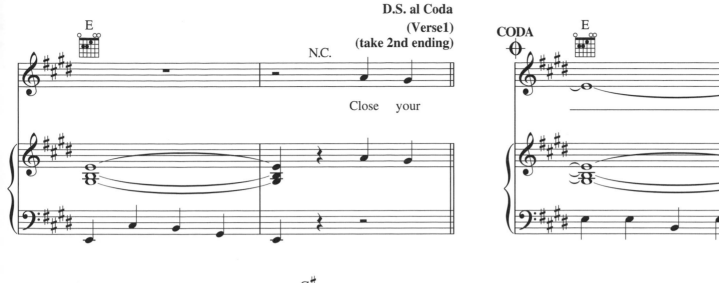

**D.S. al Coda**
**(Verse1)**
**(take 2nd ending)**

CODA

Close your

All my lov - ing, _____ all my

lov - ing, _____ ooh, _____ all my lov - ing _____

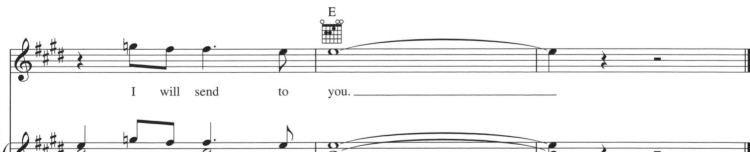

I will send to you. _____

# I WANT TO HOLD YOUR HAND

Words and Music by JOHN LENNON
and PAUL McCARTNEY

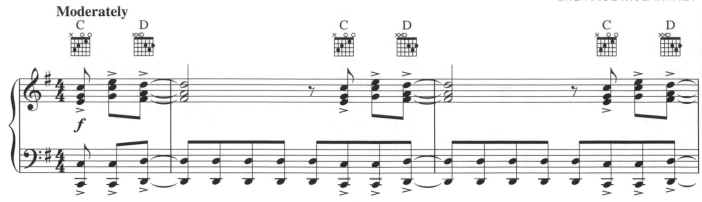

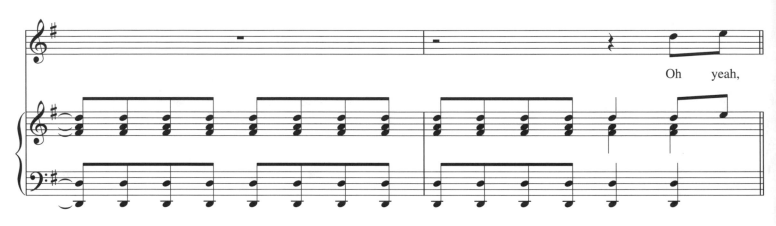

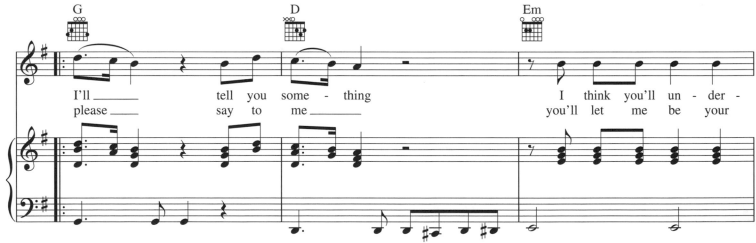

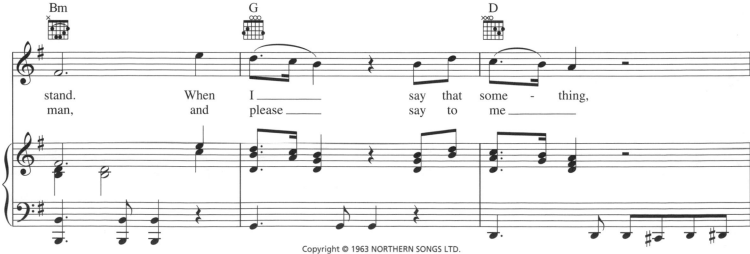

I want to hold your hand, ___
you'll let me hold your hand. ___

I want to hold your
Now let me hold your

hand, _____
hand, _____

I want to hold your hand. ___
I want to hold your

Oh, ___

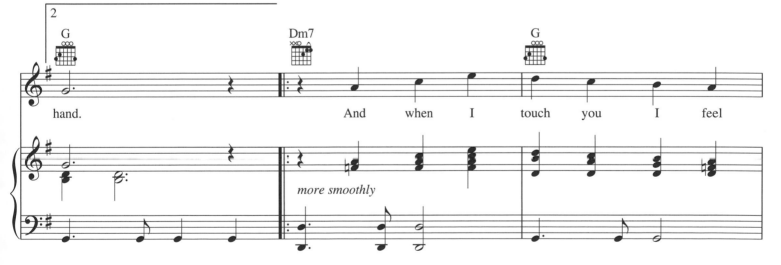

hand.

And when I touch you I feel

*more smoothly*

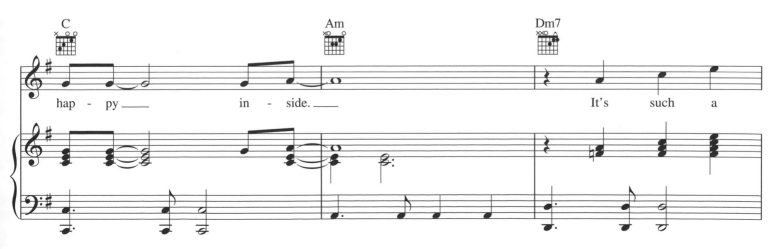

hap - py ___ in - side. ___

It's such a

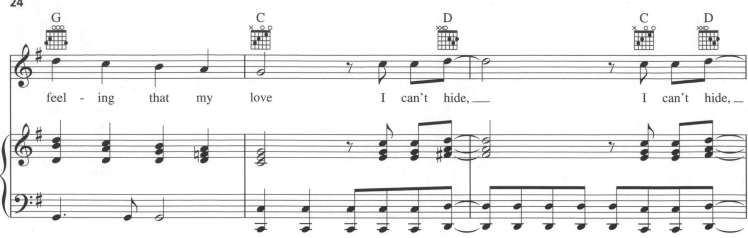

feel - ing that my love I can't hide, ___ I can't hide, ___

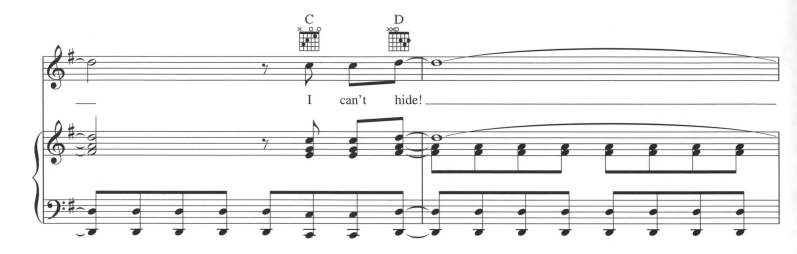

I can't hide! _____

Yeah, you _____ got that some - thing
Yeah, you _____ got that some - thing

*as before*

I think you'll un - der - stand. When I _____ say that
I think you'll un - der - stand. When I _____ feel that

# WITH A LITTLE HELP FROM MY FRIENDS

Words and Music by JOHN LENNON
and PAUL McCARTNEY

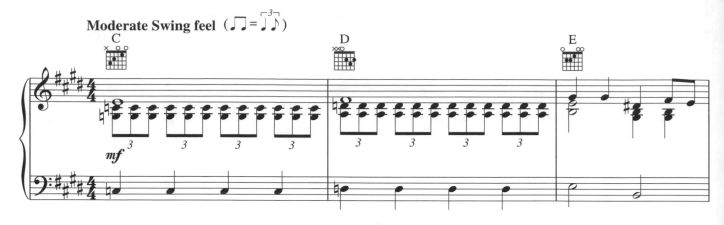

What would you think _ if I sang _ out of tune, _ would you stand _
What do I do _ when my love _ is a-way? (Does it wor- _
(Would you be-lieve _ in a love _ at first sight?) _ Yes, I'm cer-

_ up and walk _ out on me? _____
-ry you to be a-lone?) _____
-tain that it hap-pens all the time.

Lend me your ears _ and I'll sing _
How do I feel _ by the end _
(What do you see _ when you turn

you a song, ___ and I'll try _____ not to sing ___ out of key. ___
of the day? ___ (Are you sad _____ be - cause you're on your own?) _
out the light?) _ I can't tell _____ you, but I know it's mine. _

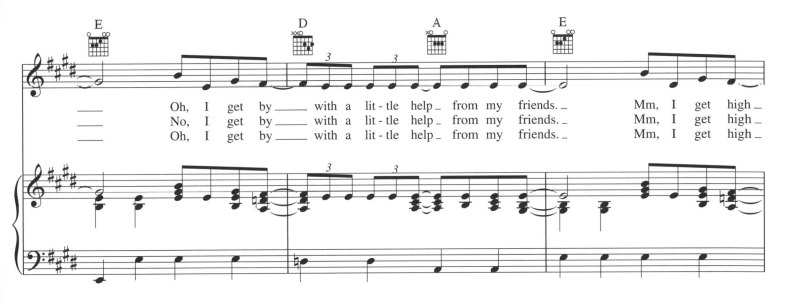

Oh, I get by ___ with a lit - tle help _ from my friends. _ Mm, I get high _
No, I get by ___ with a lit - tle help _ from my friends. _ Mm, I get high _
Oh, I get by ___ with a lit - tle help _ from my friends. _ Mm, I get high _

___ with a lit - tle help ___ from my friends. ___ Mm, I'm gon - na try ___
___ with a lit - tle help ___ from my friends. ___ Mm, I'm gon - na try ___
___ with a lit - tle help ___ from my friends. ___ Oh, I'm gon - na try ___

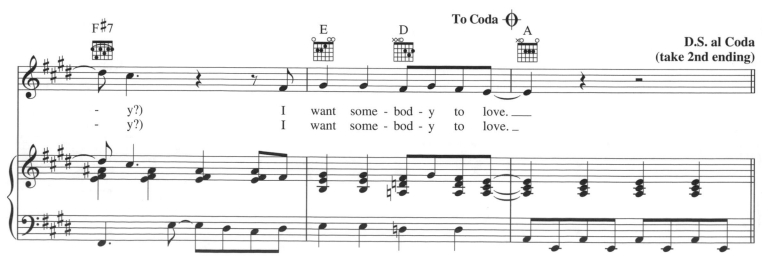

# IT WON'T BE LONG

Words and Music by JOHN LENNON
and PAUL McCARTNEY

It won't be long, yeah, (Yeah) yeah, (Yeah) yeah, (Yeah) It won't be

long, _ yeah, (Yeah) yeah, (Yeah) yeah, (Yeah) It won't be long, yeah, (Yeah) till

I be-long to you.

Ev - 'ry night when ev - 'ry - bod - y has
Ev - 'ry night the tears come down ___ from my
ev - 'ry day we'll be hap - py I

fun,
eyes,
know,

here am I
ev - 'ry day
now I know that

sit - ting all ___ on my own. )
I've done noth - ing but cry.
you won't leave ___ me no more. )

It won't be long, yeah, (Yeah) yeah, (Yeah) yeah, (Yeah) It won't be

To Coda

long,_ yeah, (Yeah) yeah, (Yeah) yeah, (Yeah) It won't be long, yeah, (Yeah) till

I be - long to you. Since you

left me I'm so a - lone,___ now you're

com - ing, you're com - ing on home.___

I'll be good like I know I should, __ you're com - ing

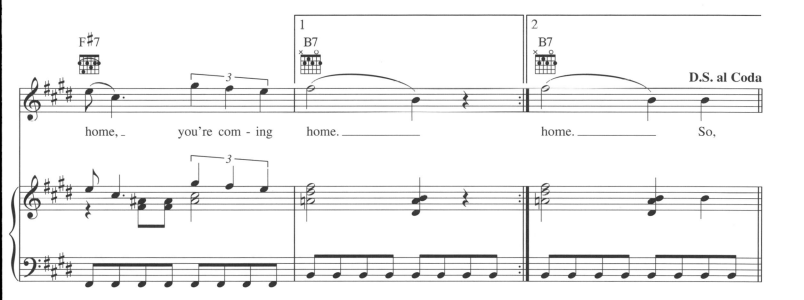

home, _ you're com - ing home. ____ home. ____ So,

D.S. al Coda

**Slowly**

**CODA**

I be - long to ____ you. ____

*rit.*

# I'VE JUST SEEN A FACE

Words and Music by JOHN LENNON
and PAUL McCARTNEY

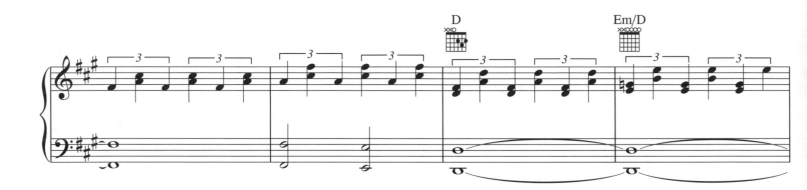

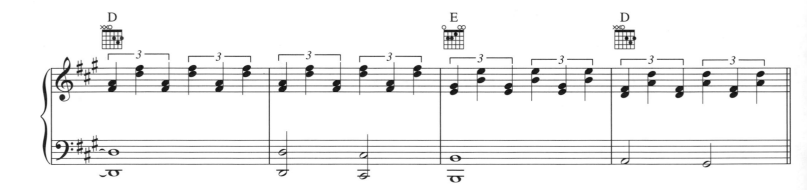

I've just seen a face, I can't for-get the time ___ or

a - ware. ___ But, as it is, I'll dream of her ___ to - night, ___
of sight, ___ for oth - er girls were nev - er quite ___ like this, ___

D E A

___ da da da da da da. ___
da da da da da da. ___
*End instrumental*

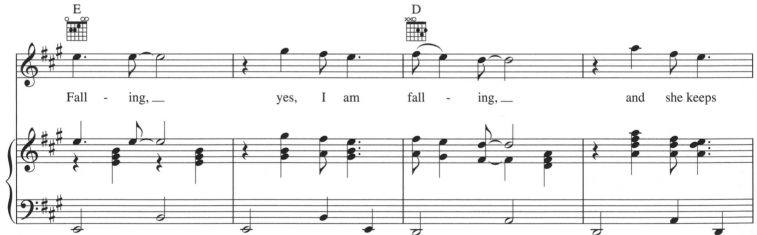

E D

Fall - ing, ___ yes, I am fall - ing, ___ and she keeps

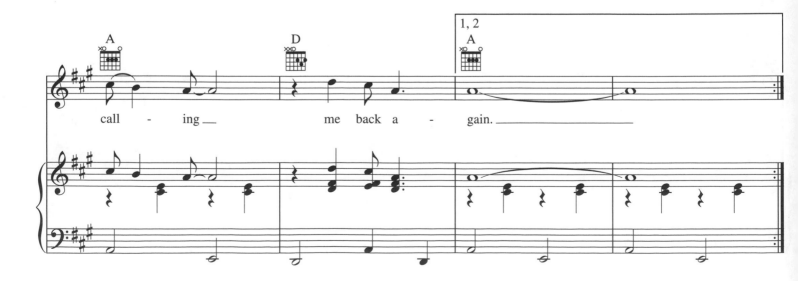

A D 1, 2 A

call - ing ___ me back a - gain. _____

# COME TOGETHER

Words and Music by JOHN LENNON
and PAUL McCARTNEY

**Moderately slow, with a double-time feeling**

Here come old flat-top, he come groov-ing up slow-ly, he got Joo Joo eye-ball, he one ho-ly roll-er, he got hair down to his knee. __ Got to be a jok-er, he just do what he please. __

He wear no shoe-shine, he got toe - jam foot-ball, he got
He Bag Pro - duc - tion, he got wal - rus gum-boot, he got
He roll - er coast-er, he got ear - ly warn - ing, he got

mon - key fin - ger, he shoot Co - ca Co - la, he say, "I know _ you,
O - no side-board, he one spi - nal crack-er, he got feet down be - low _
mud - dy wa - ter, he one Mo - jo fil - ter, he say, "One and one and one _

you know me." _
_ his knee. _
_ is three." _

One thing I can tell you is you got to be free. _ ⎫
Hold you in his arm-chair, you can feel his dis - ease. _ ⎬ Come to-geth-
Got to be good-look-ing 'cause he so hard to see. _ ⎭

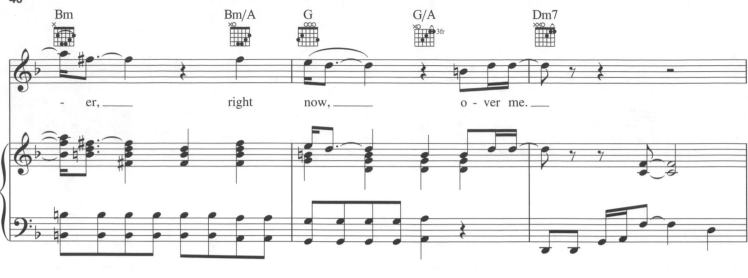

- er, \_\_\_\_ right now, \_\_\_\_ o - ver me. \_\_\_\_

**Repeat and Fade**

Come to-geth - er, \_\_\_\_

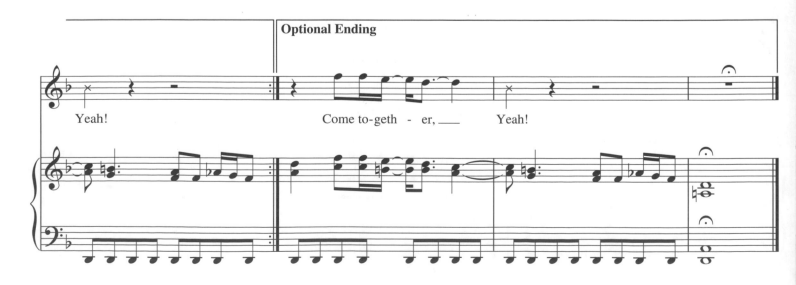

**Optional Ending**

Yeah! Come to-geth - er, \_\_\_\_ Yeah!

# DEAR PRUDENCE

Words and Music by JOHN LENNON
and PAUL McCARTNEY

Dear _____ Pru - dence, _____
_____ Pru - dence, _____
_____ Pru - dence, _____

won't you come out to play? _____
o - pen up _____ your eyes. _____
let me see _____ you smile. _____

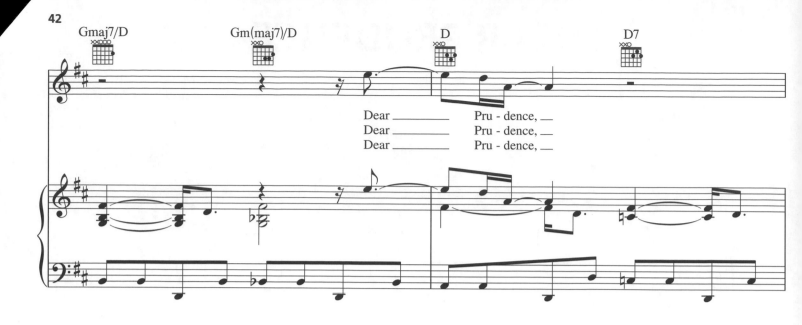

Dear _____ Pru - dence, __
Dear _____ Pru - dence, __
Dear _____ Pru - dence, __

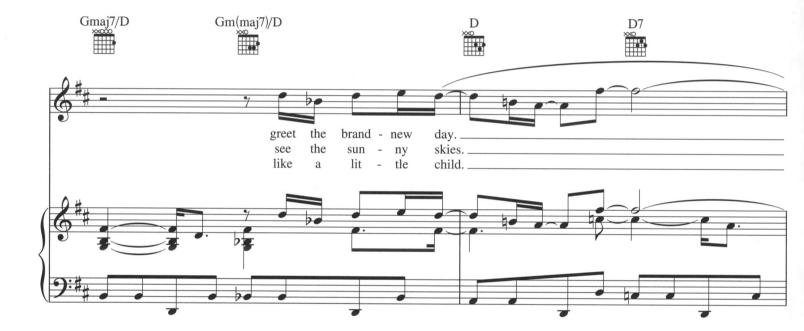

greet the brand - new day. _____
see the sun - ny skies. _____
like a lit - tle child. _____

_____

The sun is up, __ the sky is blue, __ it's
The wind is low, __ the birds will sing, __ that
The clouds will be __ a dai - sy chain, __ so

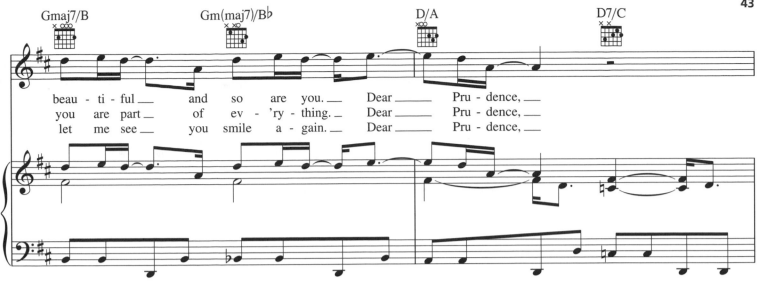

beau - ti - ful ___ and so are you. ___ Dear ___ Pru - dence, ___
you are part ___ of ev - 'ry - thing. ___ Dear ___ Pru - dence, ___
let me see ___ you smile a - gain. ___ Dear ___ Pru - dence, ___

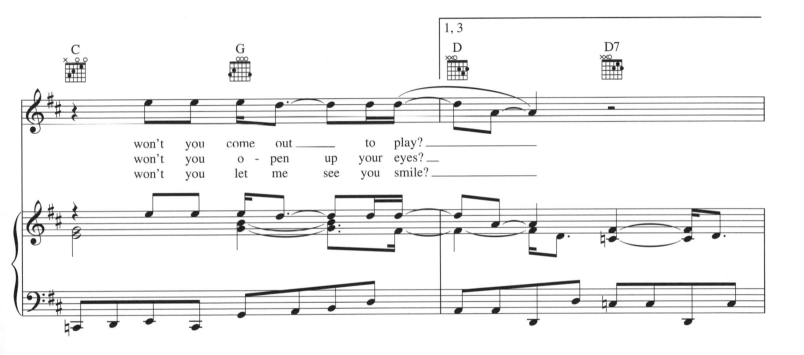

won't you come out ___ to play? ___
won't you o - pen up your eyes? ___
won't you let me see you smile? ___

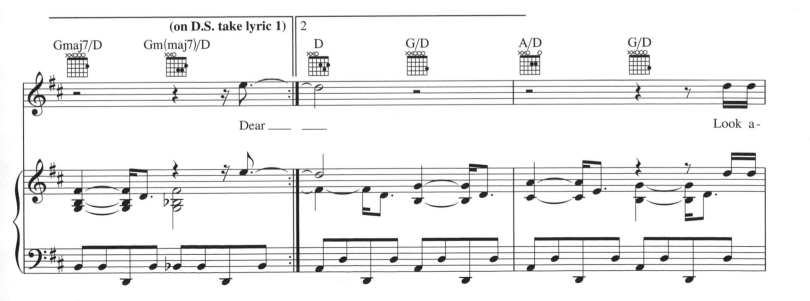

Dear ___ ___

Look a-

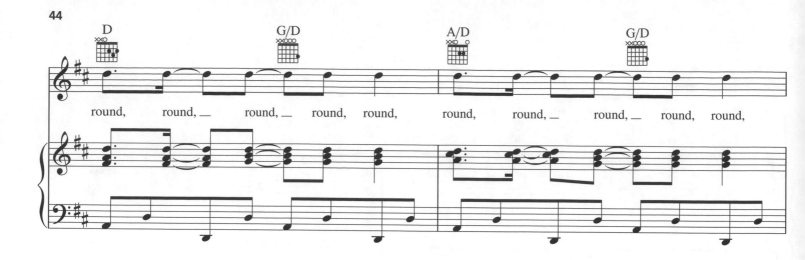

round, round, — round, — round, round, round, round, — round, — round, round,

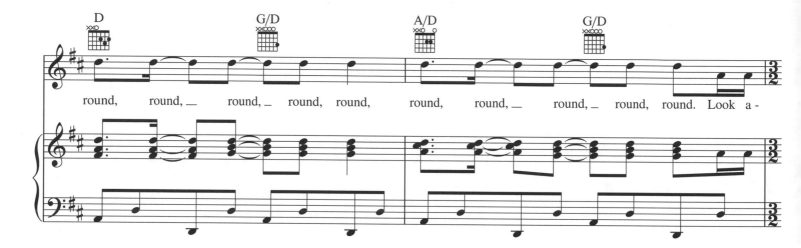

round, round, — round, — round, round, round, round, — round, — round, round. Look a-

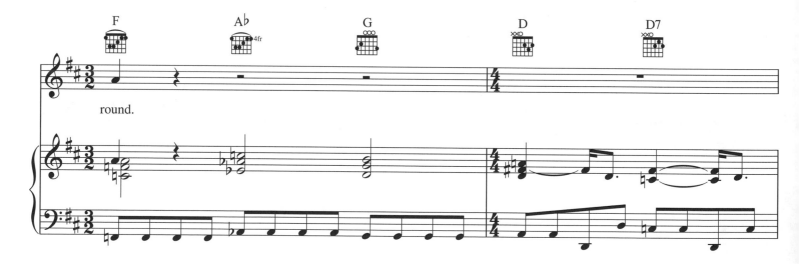

round.

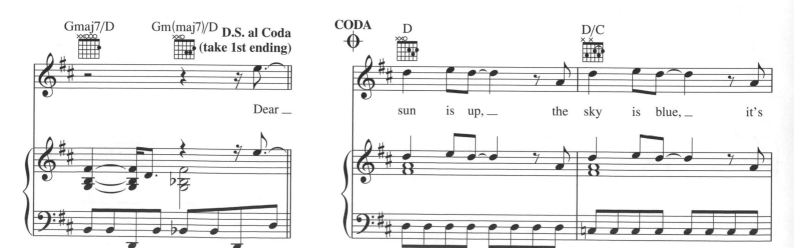

**D.S. al Coda (take 1st ending)**

Dear —

**CODA**

sun is up, — the sky is blue, — it's

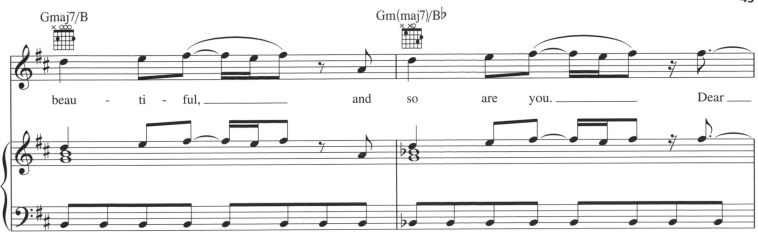

beau - ti - ful, _____ and so are you. _____ Dear _____

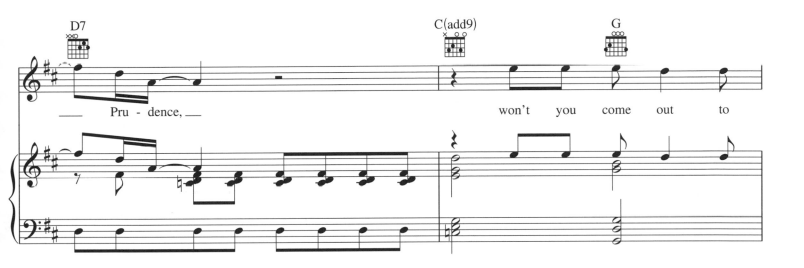

_____ Pru - dence, _____ won't you come out to

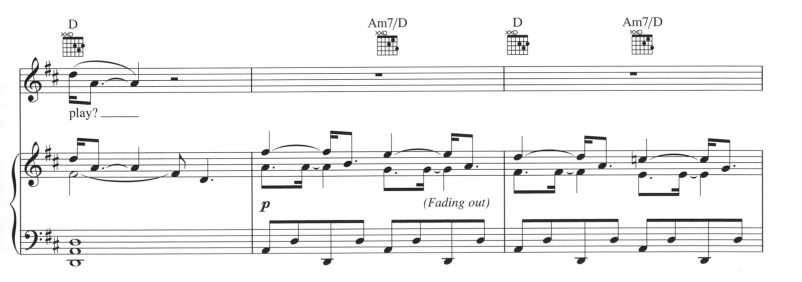

play? _____

*p*   *(Fading out)*

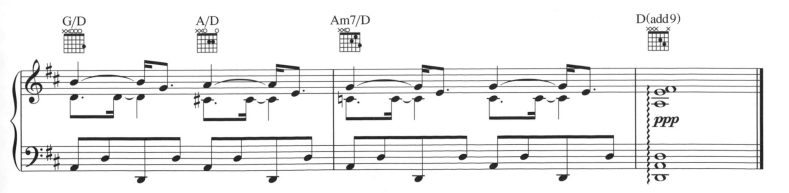

*ppp*

# IF I FELL

Words and Music by JOHN LENNON
and PAUL McCARTNEY

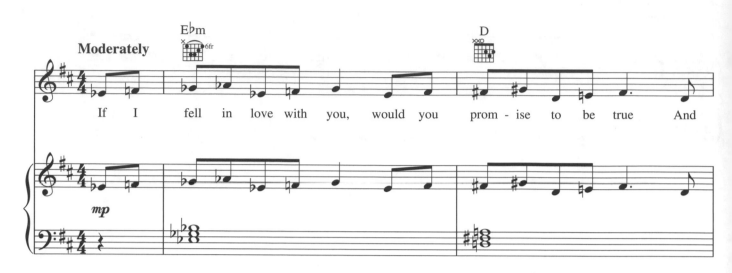

If I fell in love with you, would you prom-ise to be true And

help me un-der-stand? 'Cause I've been in love be-fore, And I

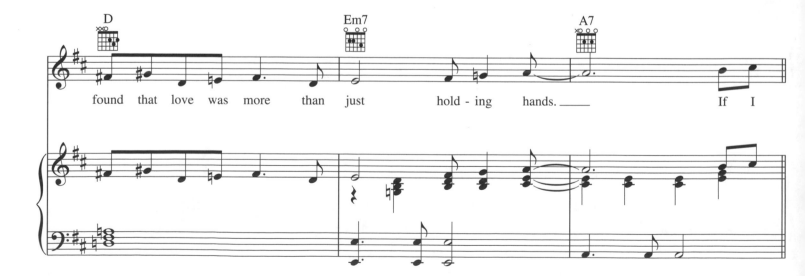

found that love was more than just hold-ing hands. ___ If I

give my heart to you, I
trust in you, oh please, don't

must be sure from the ver - y start, that
run and hide, if I love you, too, oh

**1**

you would love me more than her.
please, don't hurt my pride like

**2**

If I her. 'Cause I

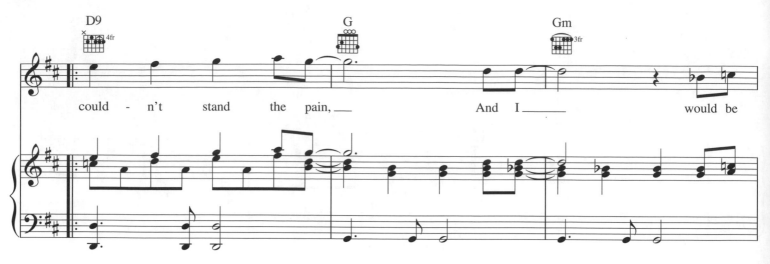

could-n't stand the pain, ___ And I ___ would be

sad if our new love was in vain. So I

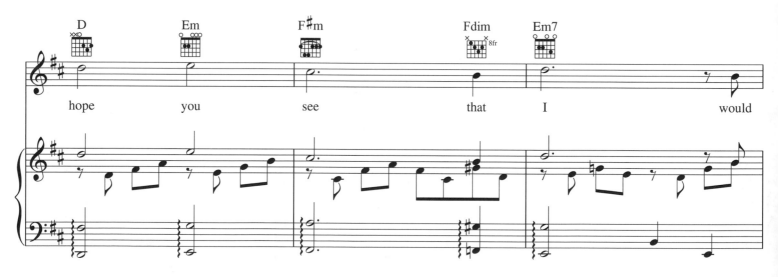

hope you see that I would

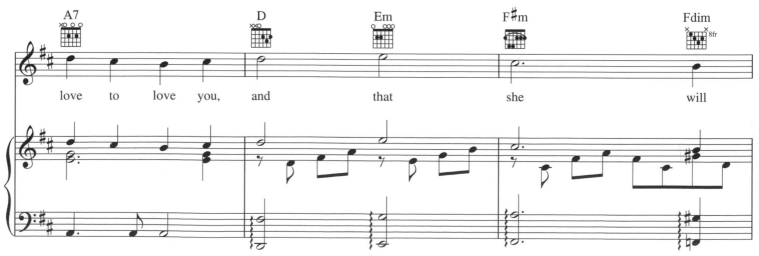

love to love you, and that she will

cry          when she learns we are two.____          'Cause I

she learns we are two.____          If I fell in love with

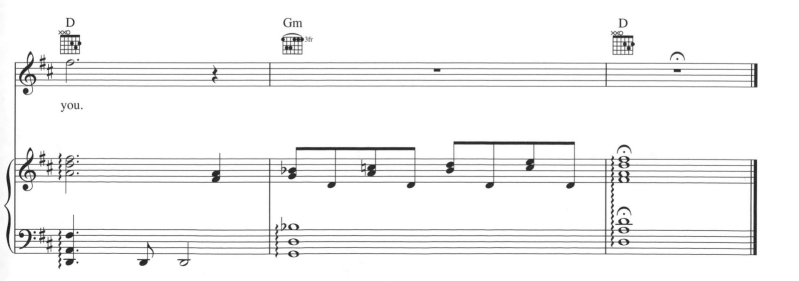

you.

# FLYING

Words and Music by JOHN LENNON,
PAUL McCARTNEY, GEORGE HARRISON
and RICHARD STARKEY

Moderately

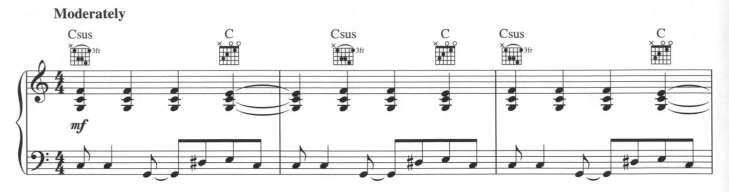

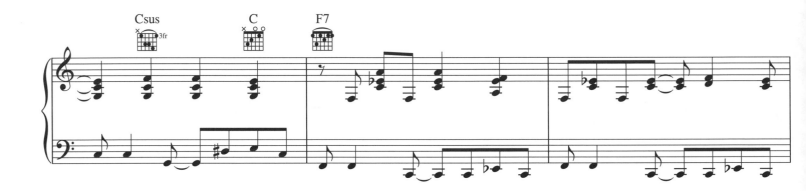

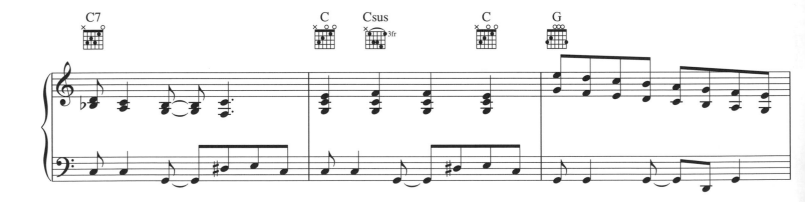

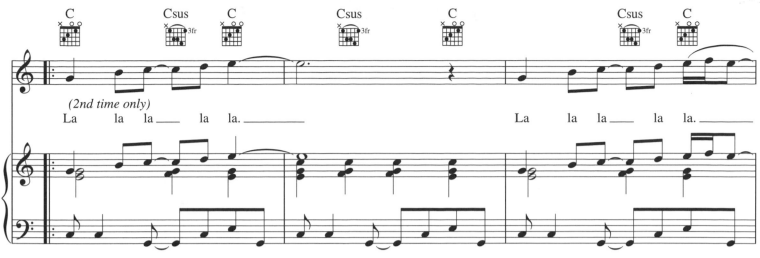

*(2nd time only)*
La la la la la. La la la la la.

La la la la la. La la la la la.

Ah, ah,

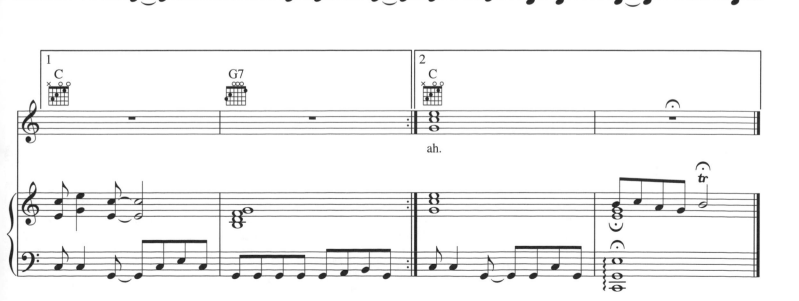

ah.

# BLUE JAY WAY

Words and Music by
GEORGE HARRISON

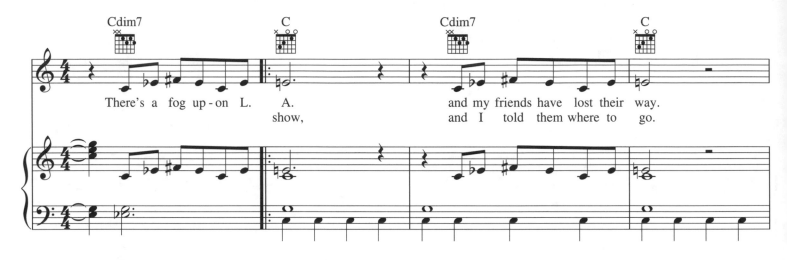

There's a fog up-on L. A. and my friends have lost their way.

show, and I told them where to go.

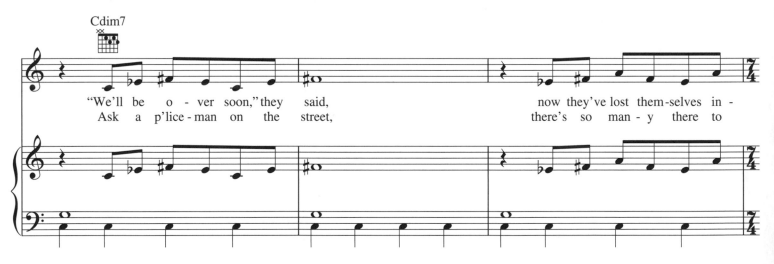

"We'll be o-ver soon," they said, now they've lost them-selves in

Ask a p'lice-man on the street, there's so man-y there to

stead. } meet. }

Please don't be long.

54

# I AM THE WALRUS

Words and Music by JOHN LENNON
and PAUL McCARTNEY

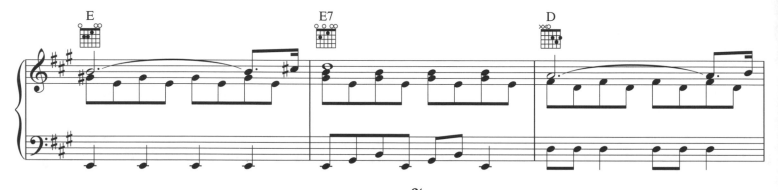

I am he as you are he as
Ex - pert tex - pert chok - ing smok - ers,

you are me and we are all to - geth - er _____
don't you think the jok - er laughs at you? _____

See how they run, like pigs from a gun, see how _____ they fly. _____ I'm
See how they smile, like pigs in a sty, see how _____ they snied. _ I'm

cry - ing. _____
cry - ing. _____

Sit - ting on a corn - flake, _____
Yel - low mat - ter cus - tard, _____
Sem - o - li - na pil - chards _____

wait - ing for the van to come. _____
drip - ping from a dead dog's eye. _____
climb - ing up the Eif - fel Tow - er. _____

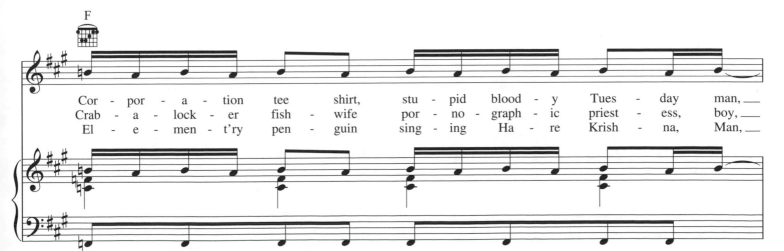

Cor - por - a - tion tee shirt, stu - pid blood - y Tues - day man, _____
Crab - a - lock - er fish - wife por - no - graph - ic priest - ess, boy, _____
El - e - men - t'ry pen - guin sing - ing Ha - re Krish - na, Man, _____

See how they fly, like Lu - cy in the sky see how __

__ they run __   I'm cry - ing. __   I'm

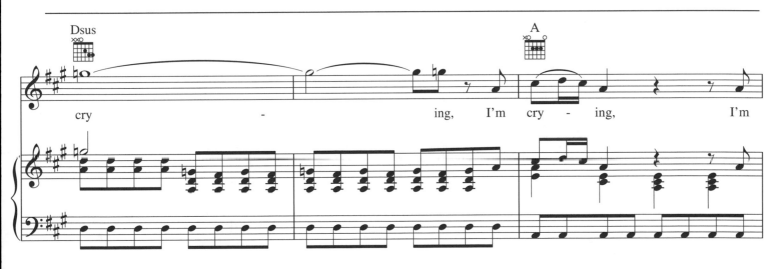

cry - ing, I'm cry - ing, I'm

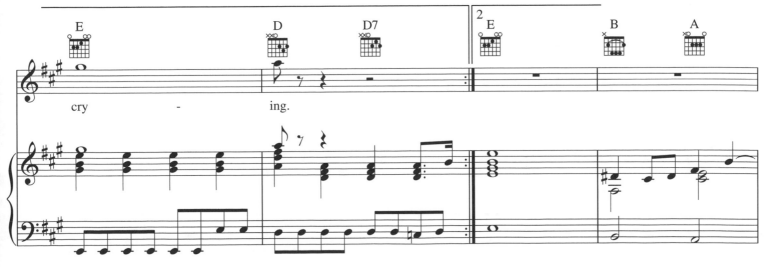

cry - ing.

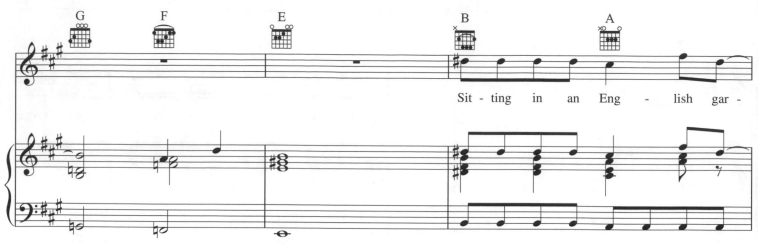

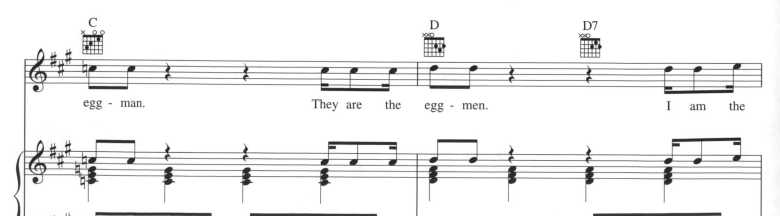

**D.S. al Coda**

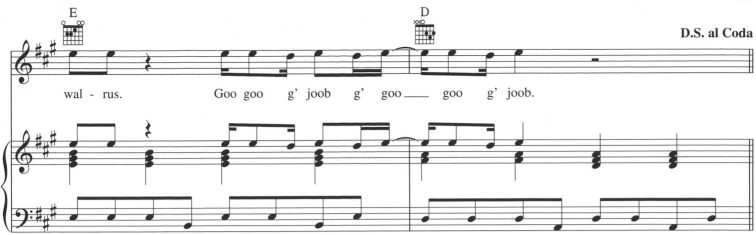

wal - rus.  Goo goo g' joob g' goo ___ goo g' joob.

**CODA**

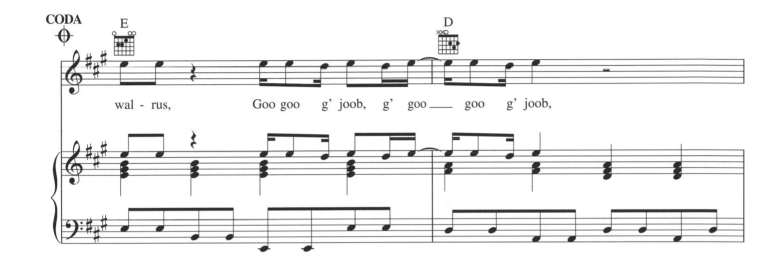

wal - rus,  Goo goo g' joob, g' goo ___ goo g' joob,

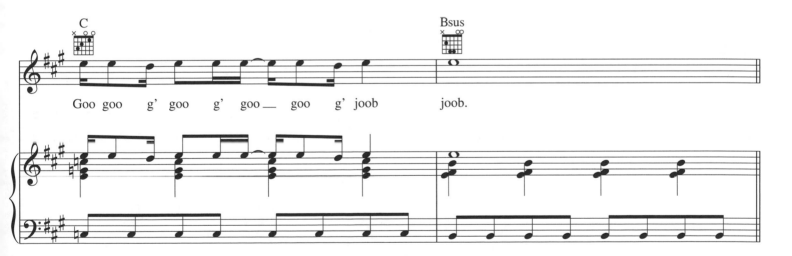

Goo goo g' goo g' goo ___ goo g' joob  joob.

**Repeat and Fade**

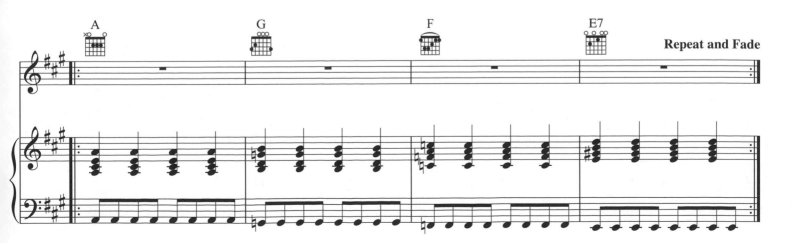

# BEING FOR THE BENEFIT OF MR. KITE

Words and Music by JOHN LENNON
and PAUL McCARTNEY

ben-e-fit of Mis-ter Kite, there will be a show to-night on tram-po-line.
cel-e-brat-ed Mis-ter K., per-forms his feat on Sat-ur-day at Bish-ops-gate.
band be-gins at ten to six when Mis-ter K. per-forms his tricks with-out a sound.

The Hen-der-sons will all be there, late of Pab-lo Fan-que's fair;
The Hen-der-sons will dance and sing as Mis-ter Kite flies through the ring;
And Mis-ter H. will dem-on-strate ten som-er-sets he'll un-der-take on

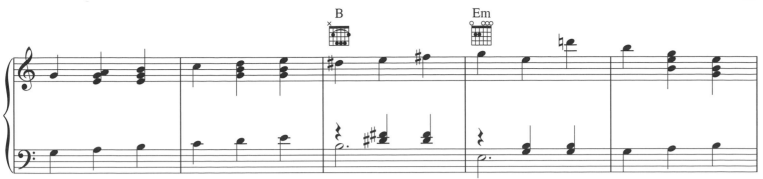

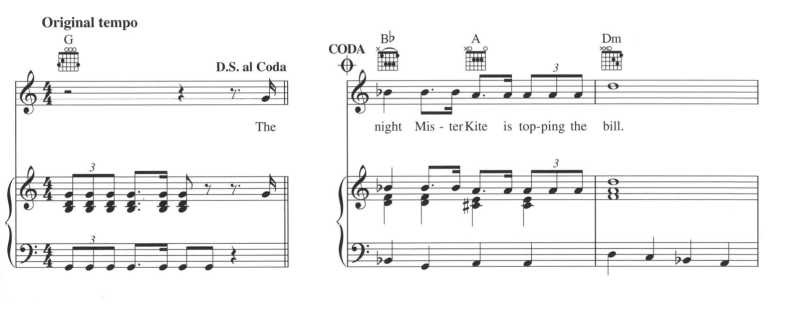

The night Mis-ter Kite is top-ping the bill.

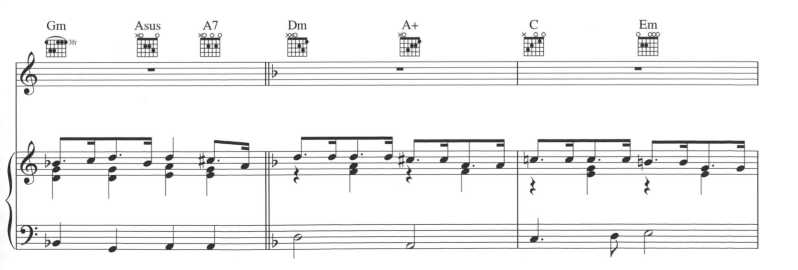

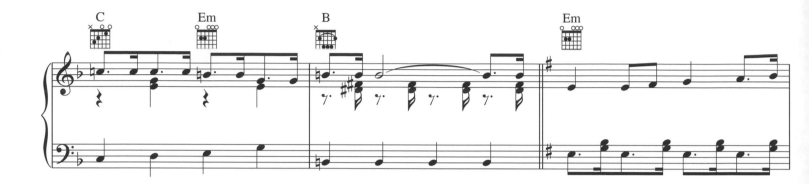

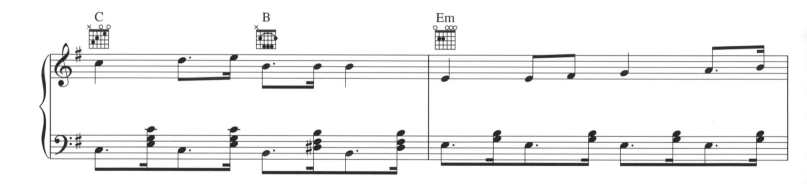

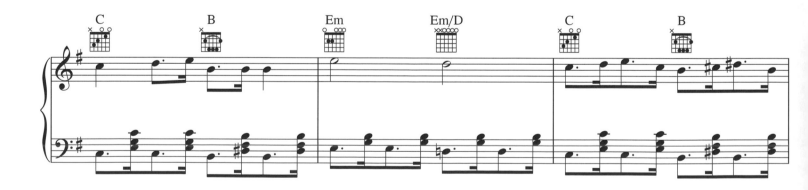

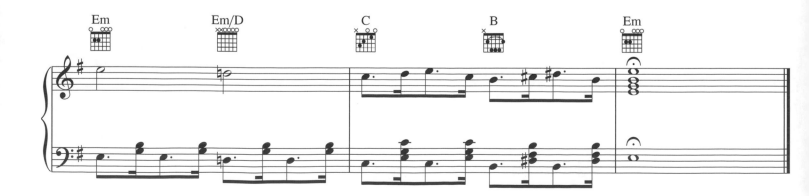

# BECAUSE

Words and Music by JOHN LENNON
and PAUL McCARTNEY

**Moderately slow**

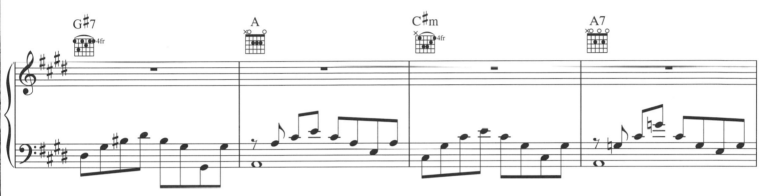

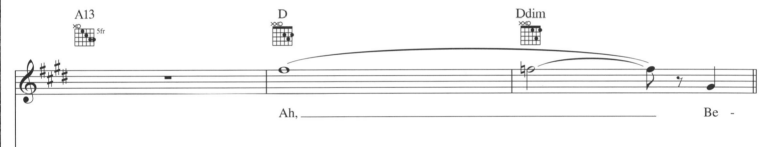

Ah, _____ Be -

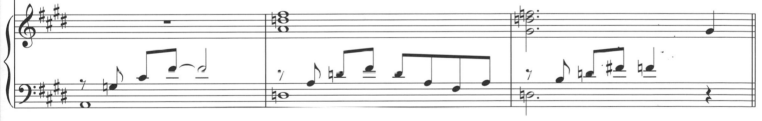

cause    the world    is    round,    it turns    me    on; ___
cause    the wind    is    high,    it blows    my    mind; ___
cause    the sky    is    blue,    it makes    me    cry; ___

be - cause _____ the world is
be - cause _____ the wind is
be - cause _____ the sky is

round. _____
high. _____
blue. _____

Ah. _____
Ah. _____

_____ Be - _____ Love is old, love is new;

love is all, love is you.

Be -

69

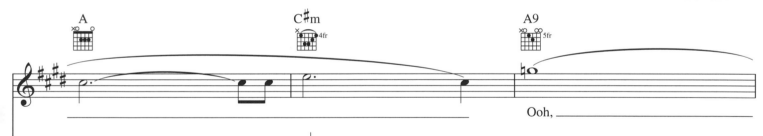

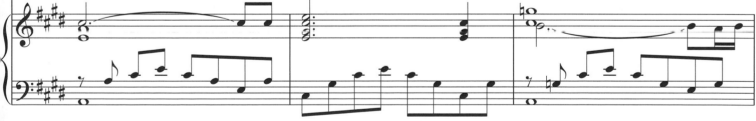

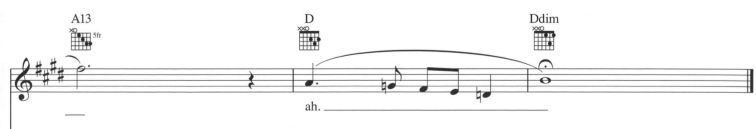

# SOMETHING

Words and Music by
GEORGE HARRISON

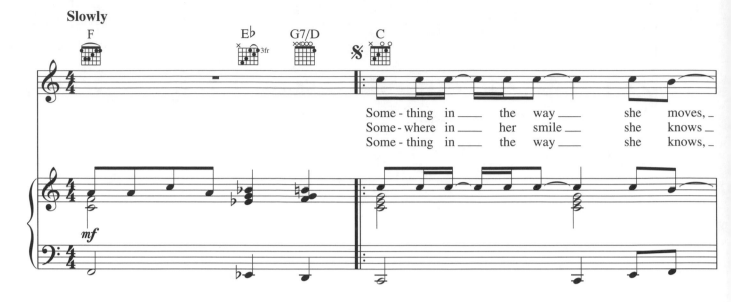

Some - thing in ___ the way ___ she moves, ___
Some - where in ___ her smile ___ she knows ___
Some - thing in ___ the way ___ she knows, ___

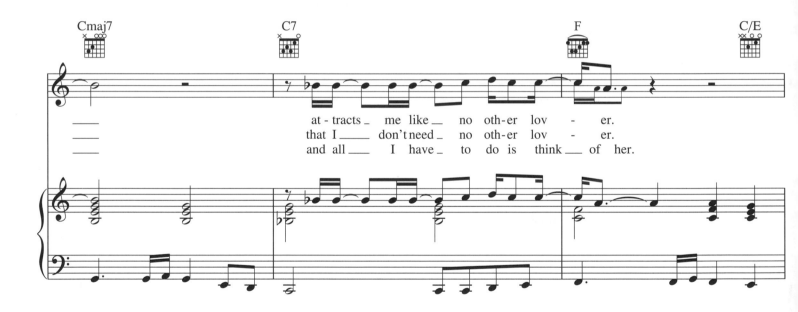

at - tracts ___ me like ___ no oth-er lov - ___ er.
that I ___ don't need ___ no oth-er lov - ___ er.
and all ___ I have ___ to do is think ___ of her.

Some-thing in ___ the way ___ she woos ___ me. ⎫
Some-thing in ___ her style ___ that shows ___ me. ⎬   I don't want to leave ___ her now,      you
Some-thing in ___ the things ___ she shows ___ me. ⎭

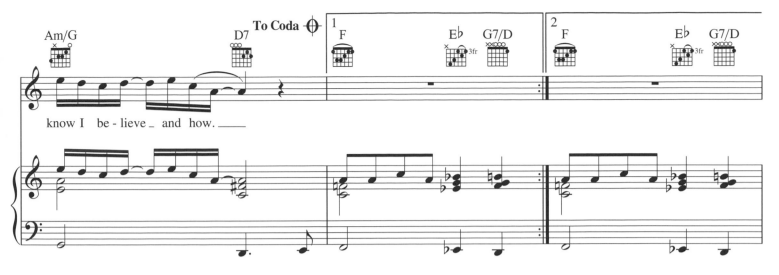

know I be-lieve ___ and how. ___

You're ask-ing me ___ will my ___ love grow, I don't know ___

___ I ___ don't know. You stick a - round ___ now, it may

show, I don't know, ___ I ___ don't know.

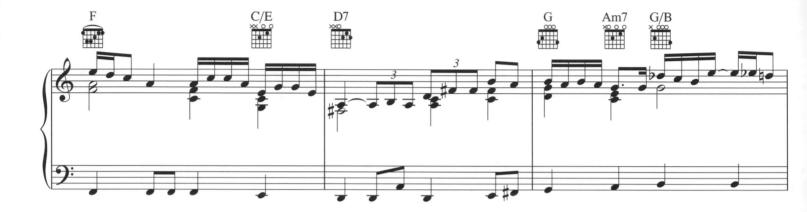

**D.S. al Coda**

# WHILE MY GUITAR GENTLY WEEPS

Words and Music by
GEORGE HARRISON

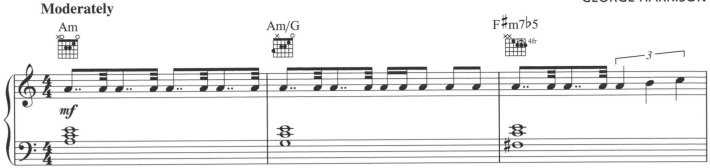

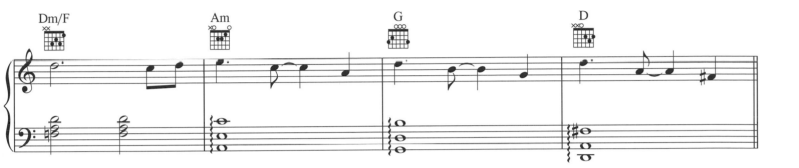

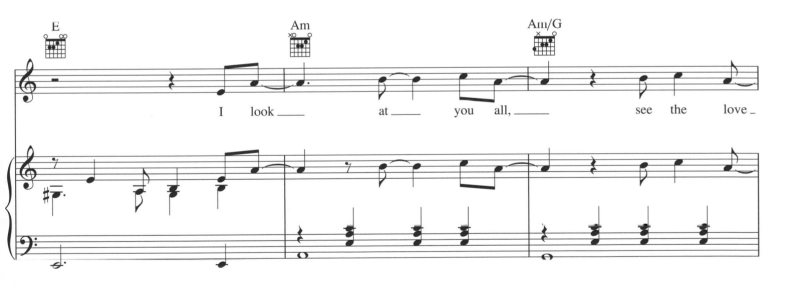

I look ___ at ___ you all, ___ see the love ___

___ there ___ that's sleep - ing ___ while my gui - tar ___ gen - tly weeps. ___

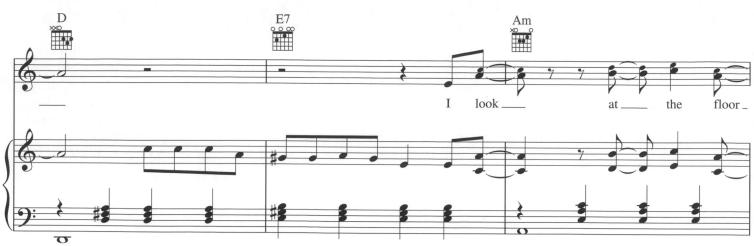

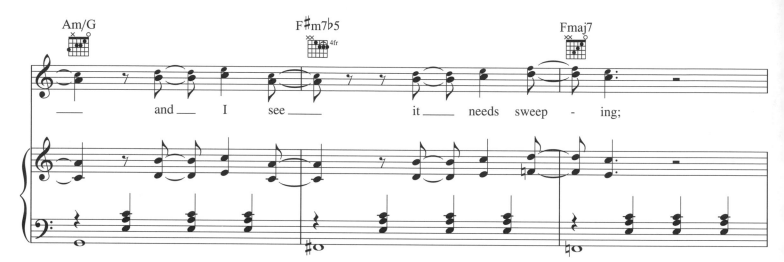

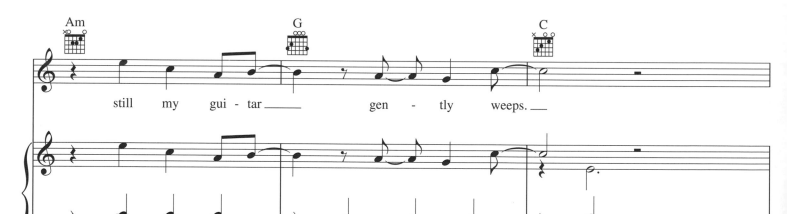

no - bod - y told ___ you
you ___ were di - vert - ed,

how ___ to un -
you ___ were per -

fold ___ your love. ___
vert - ed, too. ___

I don't know how ___
I don't know how ___

some - one con -
you ___ were in -

trolled you, ___
vert - ed, ___

they ___ bought and sold ___ you. ___
no ___ one a - lert - ed you. ___

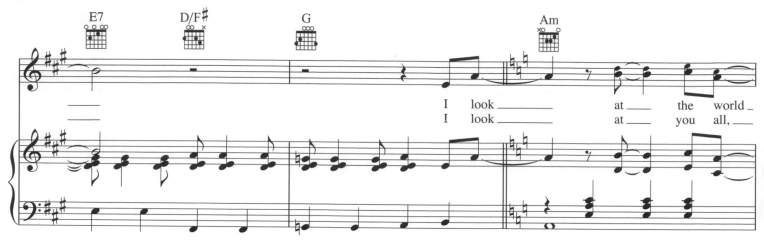

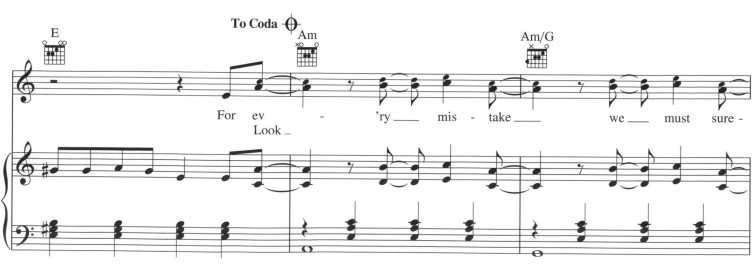

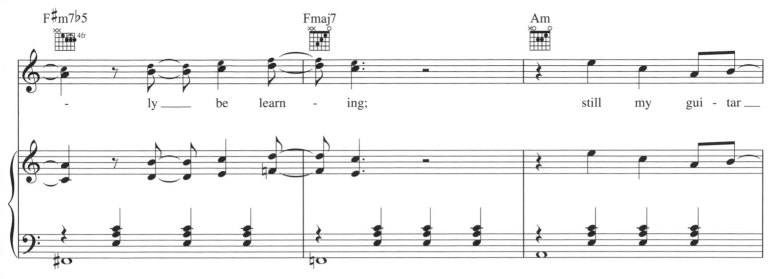

-ly ___ be learn - ing; still my gui - tar ___

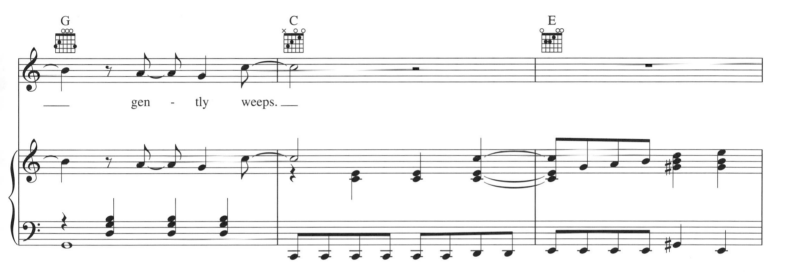

___ gen - tly weeps. ___

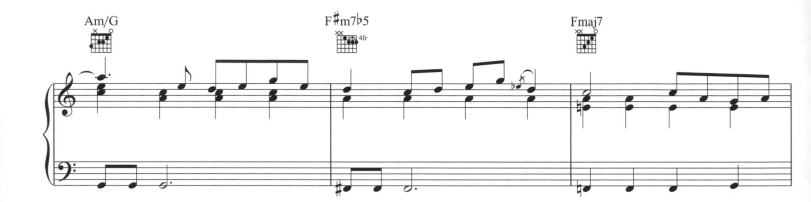

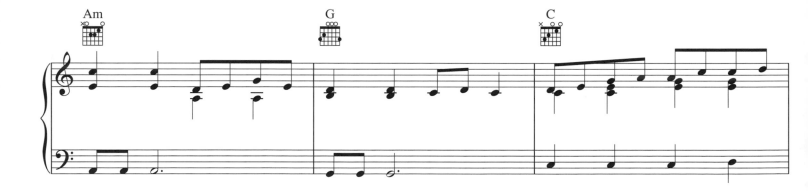

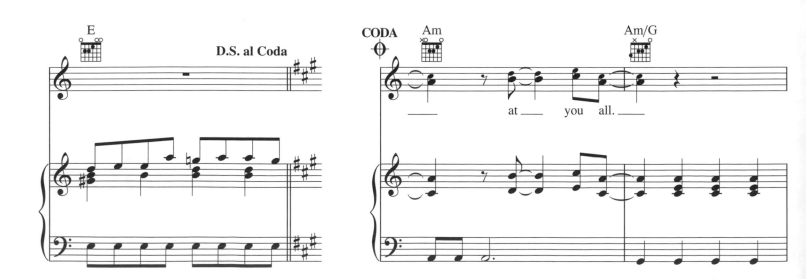

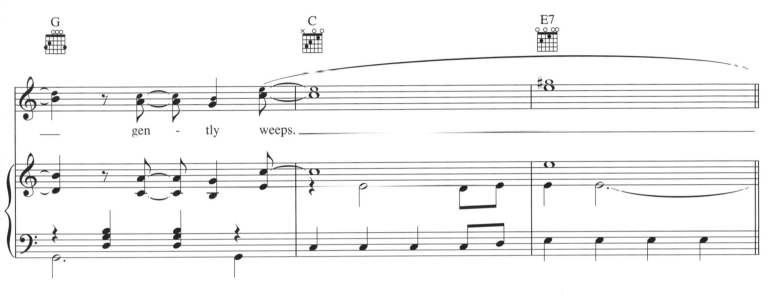

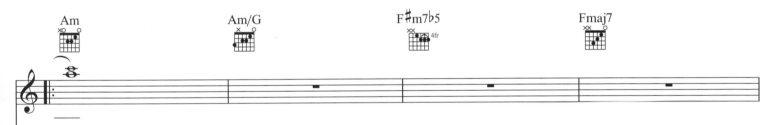

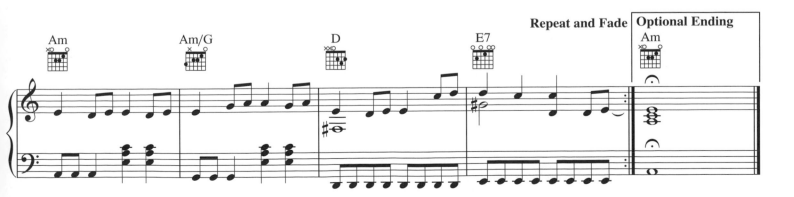

# OH! DARLING

Words and Music by JOHN LENNON
and PAUL McCARTNEY

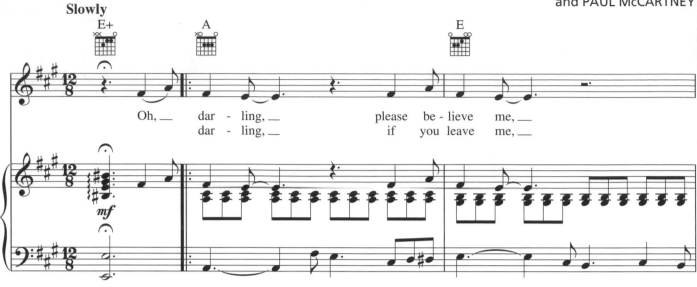

Oh, __ dar - ling, __ please be - lieve me, __
dar - ling, __ if you leave me, __

I'll nev - er do you _____ no harm; _____ be -
I'll nev - er make it _____ a - lone; _____ be -

lieve me when I tell you, I'll nev - er do you _____ no
lieve me when I beg you, don't ev - er leave me _____ a -

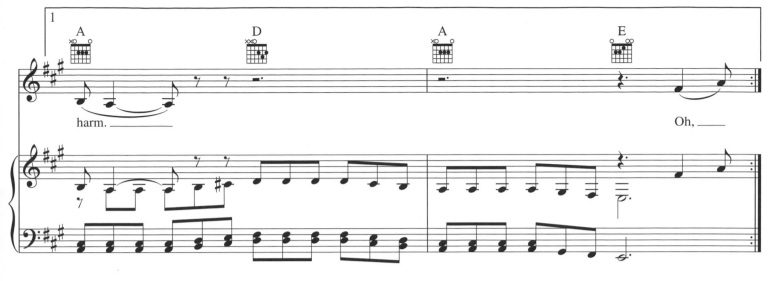

1

A    D    A    E

harm. _____                                                                Oh, _____

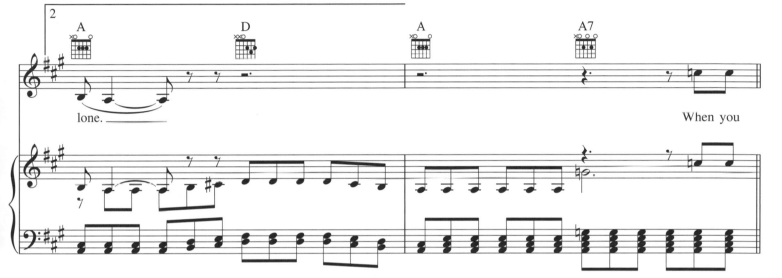

2

A    D    A    A7

lone. _____                                                            When you

D                          F7

told  me ___              you did-n't  need  me  an-y-more, ____              well, you

A

know  I  near - ly  broke  down ____  and  cried. _____              When you

told me ____ you did - n't need me an - y - more, ____ well, you

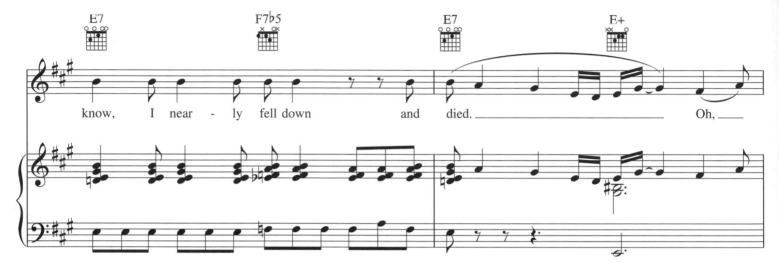

know, I near - ly fell down and died. _____ Oh, ____

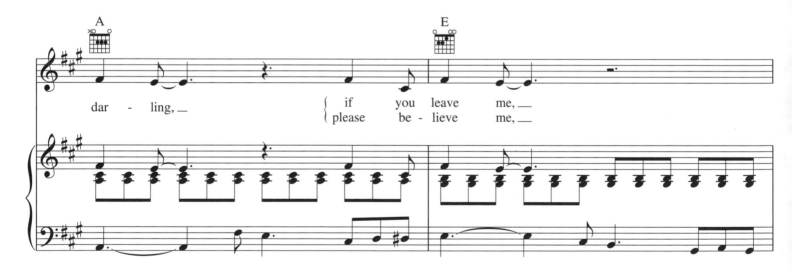

dar - ling, ____ { if you leave me, ____
{ please be - lieve me, ____

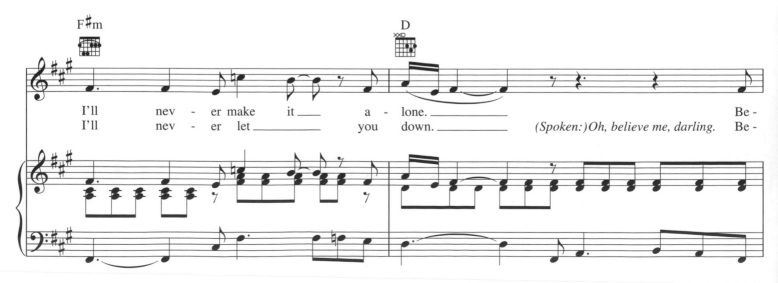

I'll nev - er make it ____ a - lone. _____ Be -
I'll nev - er let _____ you down. _____ *(Spoken:) Oh, believe me, darling.* Be -

lieve me when I tell you
lieve me when I tell you

I'll nev - er do you __ no

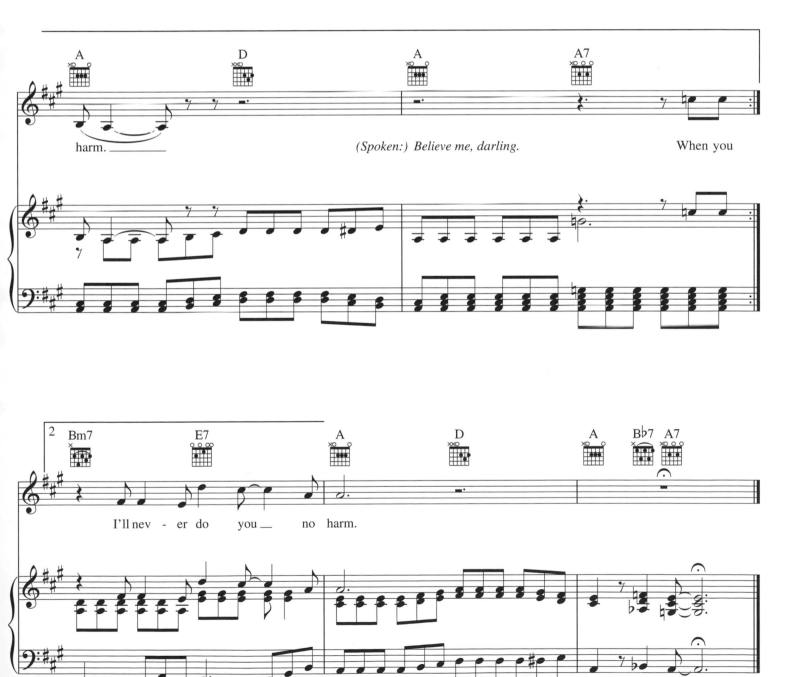

harm. _____

*(Spoken:)* Believe me, darling.

When you

I'll nev - er do you __ no harm.

# STRAWBERRY FIELDS FOREVER

Words and Music by JOHN LENNON
and PAUL McCARTNEY

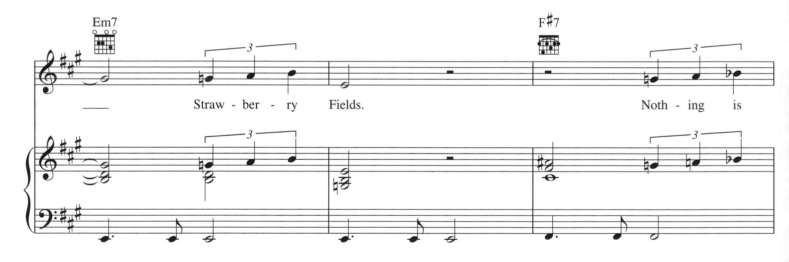

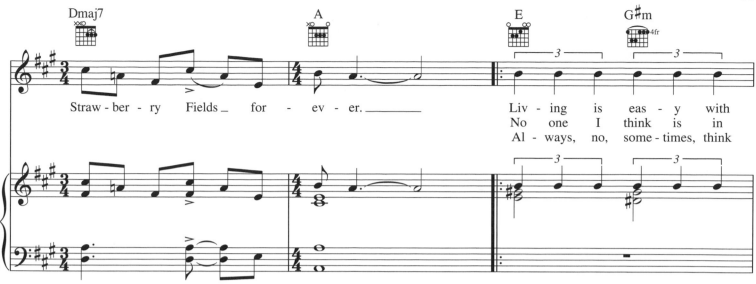

Straw - ber - ry Fields _ for - ev - er. _____  Liv - ing is eas - y with
No one I think is in
Al - ways, no, some - times, think

eyes closed, ____  mis - un - der - stand - ing all you
my tree, _____  I mean, it must be high or
it's me, _____  but you know I know when it's a

see. _____  It's get - ting hard to be some -
low. _____  That is, you can't, you know, tune
dream. _____  I think a "No," I mean a

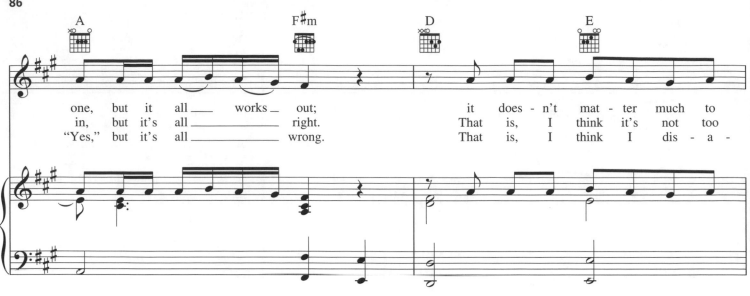

one, but it all ___ works ___ out;      it does-n't mat-ter much to
in, but it's all _____ right.      That is, I think it's not too
"Yes," but it's all _____ wrong.      That is, I think I dis-a-

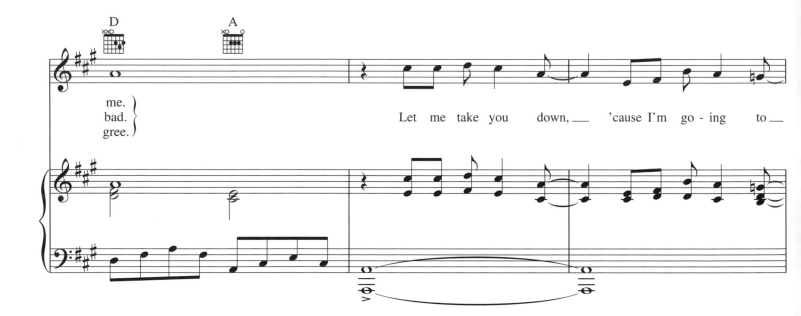

me.
bad.    Let me take you down, ___ 'cause I'm go-ing to ___
gree.

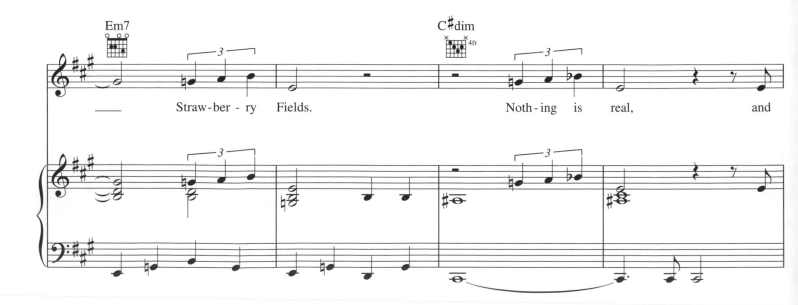

___ Straw-ber-ry Fields.      Noth-ing is real, ___ and

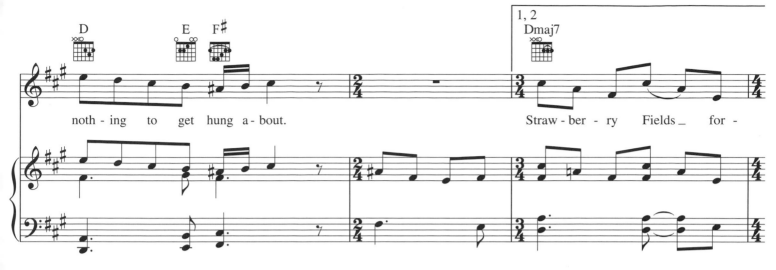

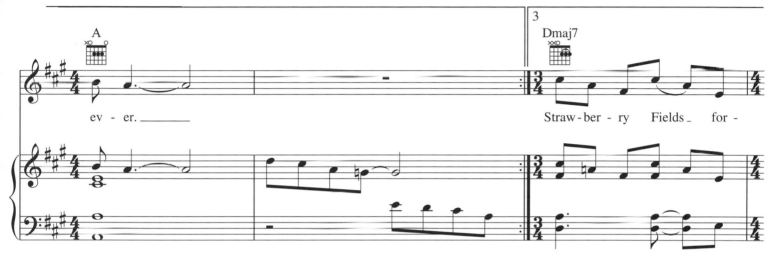

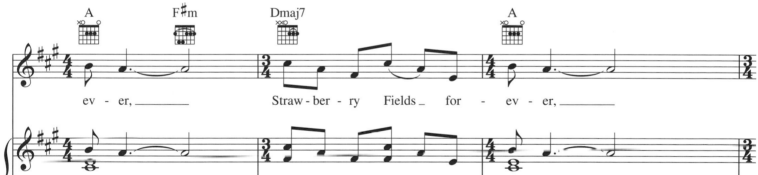

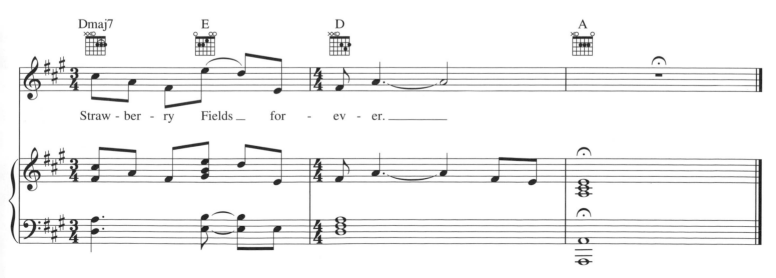

# REVOLUTION

Words and Music by JOHN LENNON
and PAUL McCARTNEY

**Moderate Rock and Roll Shuffle**

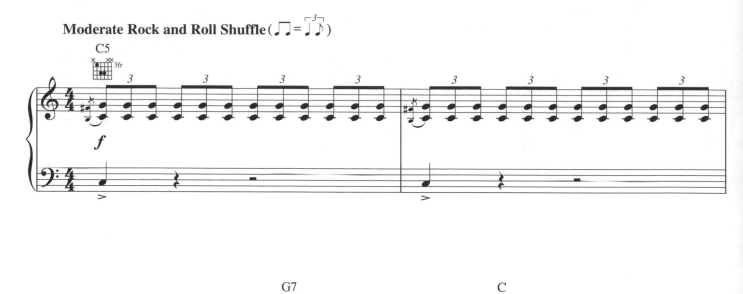

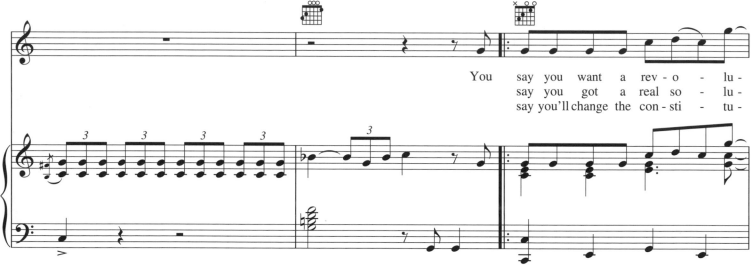

You say you want a rev-o-lu-
say you got a real so-lu-
say you'll change the con-sti-tu-

-tion; _____ well, _____ you know, _____ we all want __
-tion; _____ well, _____ you know, _____ we'd all love __
-tion; _____ well, _____ you know, _____ we all want __

to change the world.
to see the plan.
to change your head.

You
You
You

tell me that it's ev - o - lu - tion; _____ well, _____ you know, _____
ask me for a con - tri - bu - tion; _____ well, _____ you know, _____
tell me it's the in - sti - tu - tion; _____ well, _____ you know, _____

we all want _____ to change the world. _____
we're all do - ing what we can. _____
you better free _____ your mind in - stead. _____

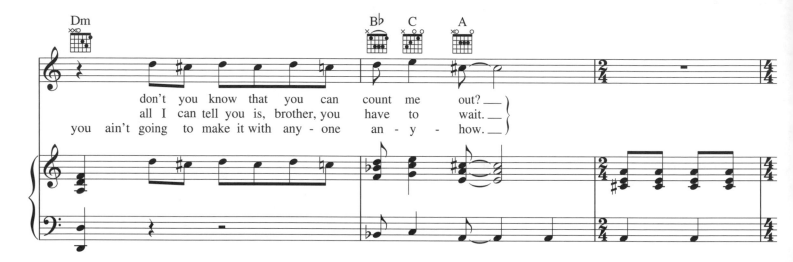

But when you talk a - bout de - struc - tion, ___
But if you want money for people with minds that hate, ___
But if you go carry - ing pictures of Chair-man Mao, ___

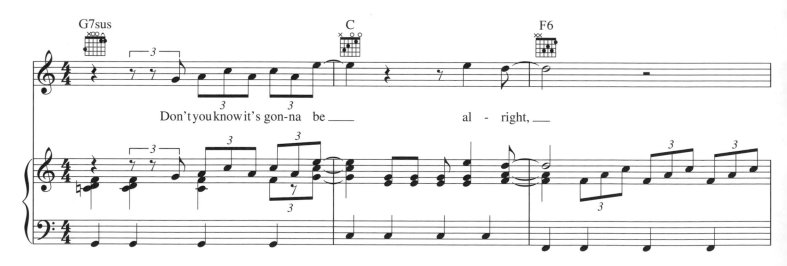

don't you know that you can count me out? ___
all I can tell you is, brother, you have to wait. ___
you ain't going to make it with any - one an - y - how. ___

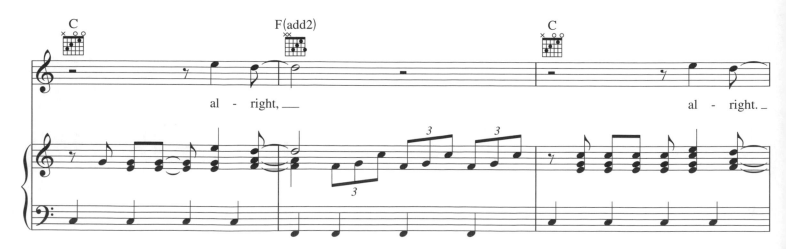

Don't you know it's gon-na be ___ al - right, ___

al - right, ___ al - right. ___

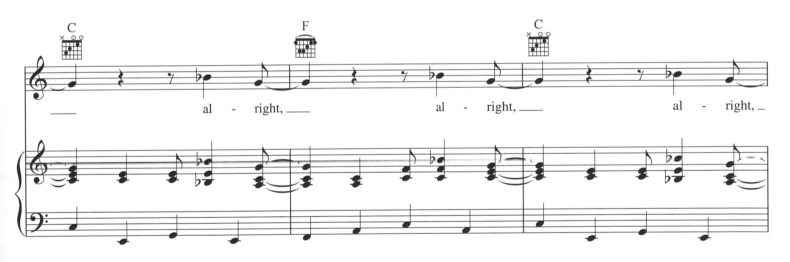

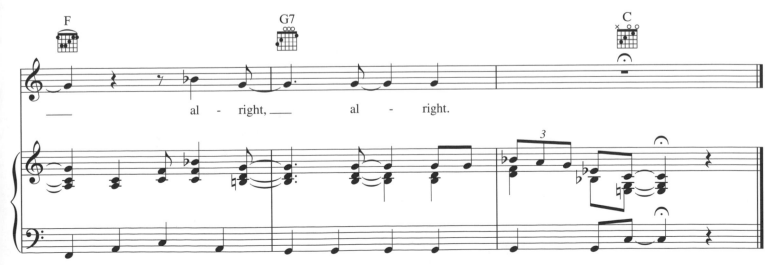

# ACROSS THE UNIVERSE

Words and Music by JOHN LENNON
and PAUL McCARTNEY

**Slowly and smoothly**

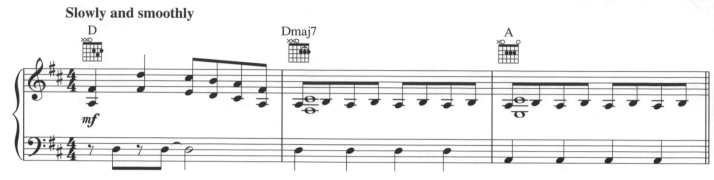

Words are flow-ing out ___ like end-less rain ___ in-to a pa-per cup, ___ they

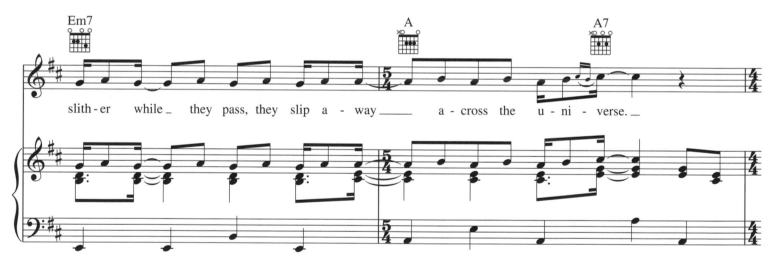

slith-er while ___ they pass, they slip a-way ___ a-cross the u-ni-verse. ___

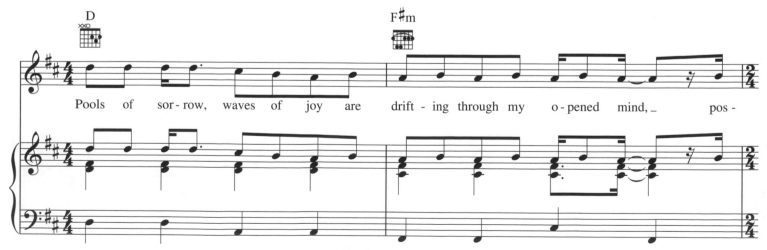

Pools of sor-row, waves of joy are drift-ing through my o-pened mind, ___ pos-

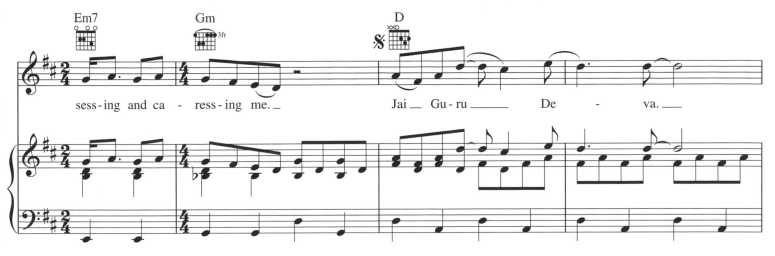

Im- ag - es___ of bro-ken light___ which dance be-fore___ me like a mil - lion eyes,_

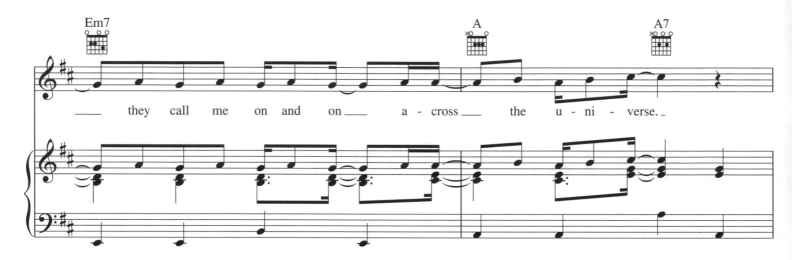

___ they call me on and on___ a-cross___ the u - ni - verse._

Thoughts me-an - der like a rest - less wind in-side a let-ter-box,___ they

D.S. al Coda

tum- ble blind-ly as they make their way a-cross_ the u - ni - verse.__

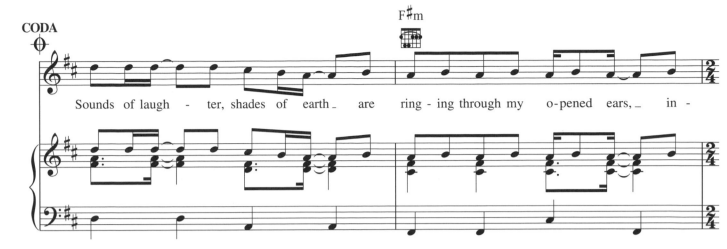

CODA

Sounds of laugh - ter, shades of earth _ are ring - ing through my o-pened ears, _ in -

cit - ing and in - vit - ing me. _ Lim-it - less, _ un-dy-ing love, _ which

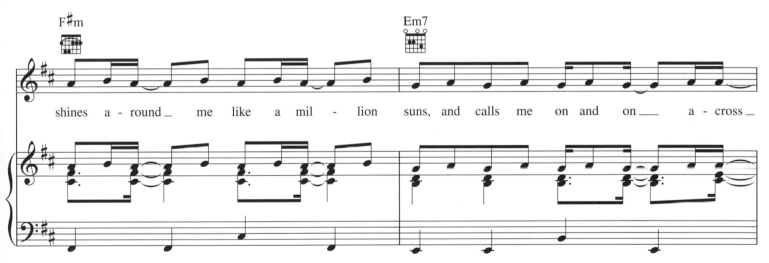

shines a - round _ me like a mil - lion suns, and calls me on and on _ a - cross _

_ the u - ni - verse. _ Jai _ Gu - ru _ De -

# HELTER SKELTER

Words and Music by JOHN LENNON
and PAUL McCARTNEY

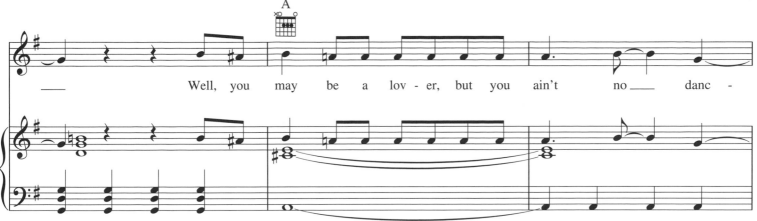

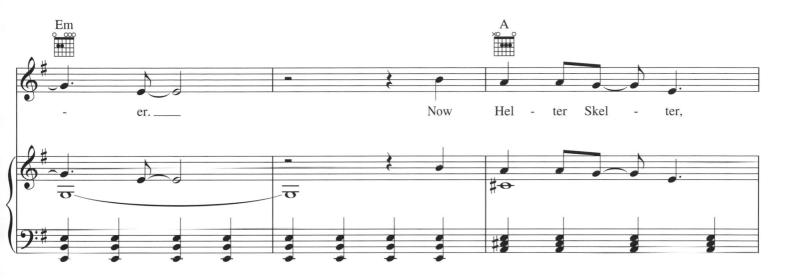

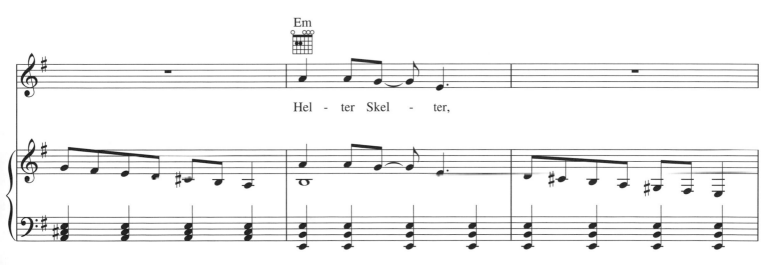

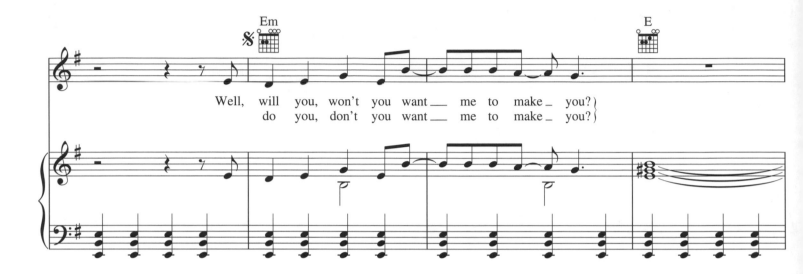

Well, will you, won't you want ___ me to make ___ you?
do you, don't you want ___ me to make ___ you?

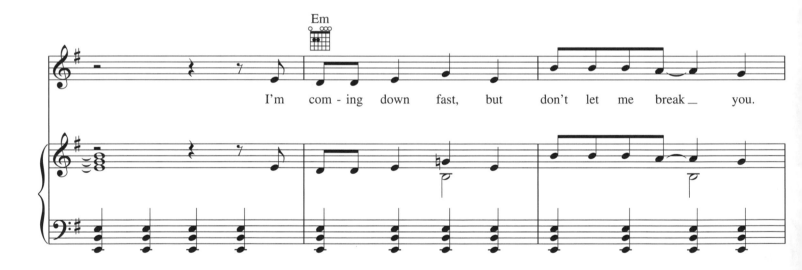

I'm com - ing down fast, but don't let me break ___ you.

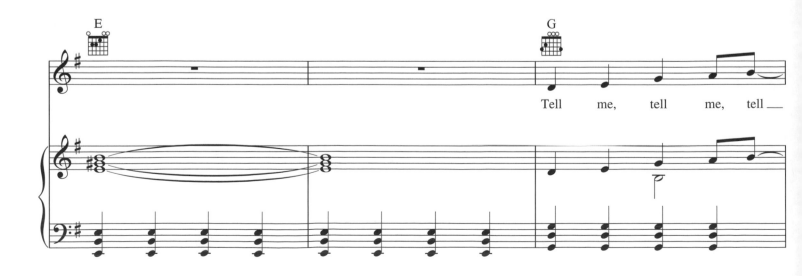

Tell me, tell me, tell ___

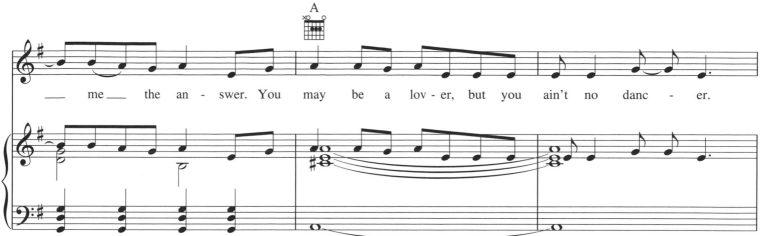

me the an-swer. You may be a lov-er, but you ain't no danc - er.

Look out! Hel - ter Skel - ter,

Hel - ter Skel - ter,

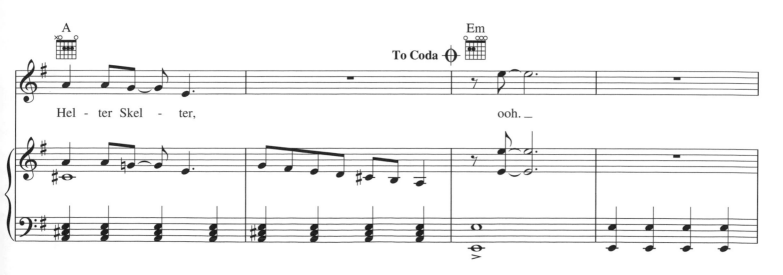

To Coda

Hel - ter Skel - ter, ooh.

Look out!          'Cause here she comes!

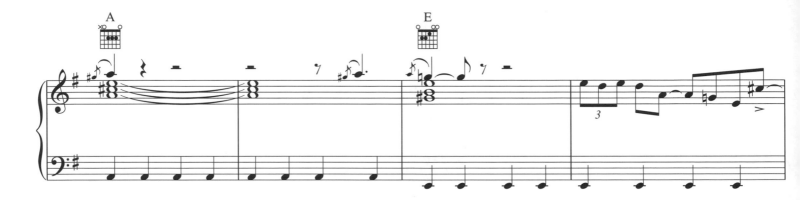

When I

get          to the bot - tom I go back          to the top of the slide, ___ and I stop    and I

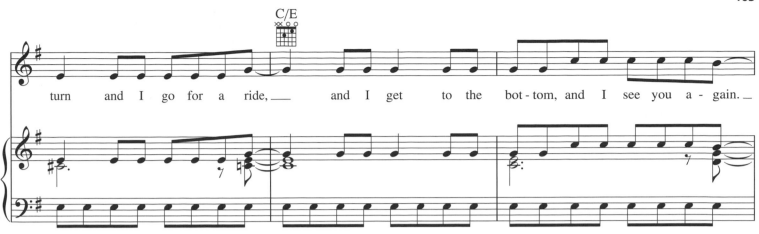

turn and I go for a ride, ___ and I get to the bot-tom, and I see you a-gain. ___

**D.S. al Coda**

Yeah, yeah, yeah, ___ yeah!

Well,

**CODA**

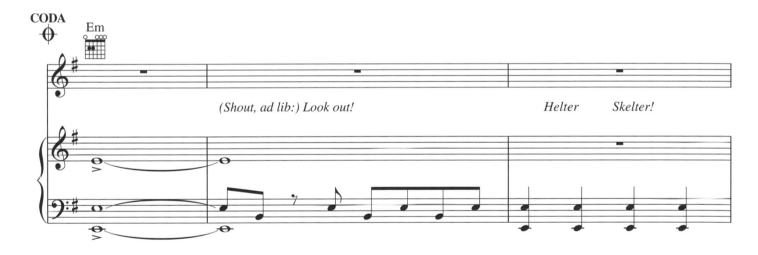

*(Shout, ad lib:)* Look out!

*Helter    Skelter!*

**Repeat ad lib. and Fade**

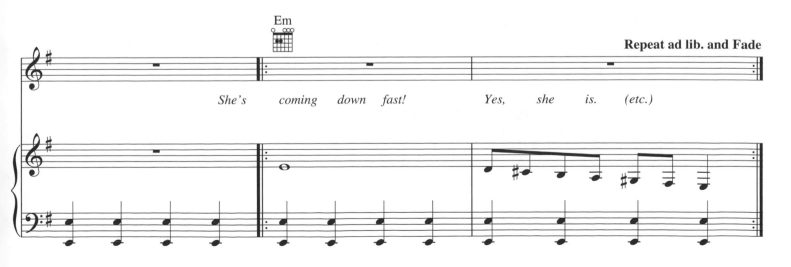

*She's    coming    down    fast!    Yes,    she    is.    (etc.)*

# HAPPINESS IS A WARM GUN

Words and Music by JOHN LENNON
and PAUL McCARTNEY

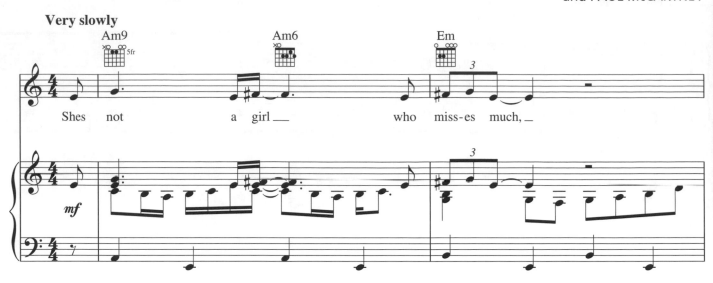

Very slowly

Shes not a girl _____ who miss-es much, _____

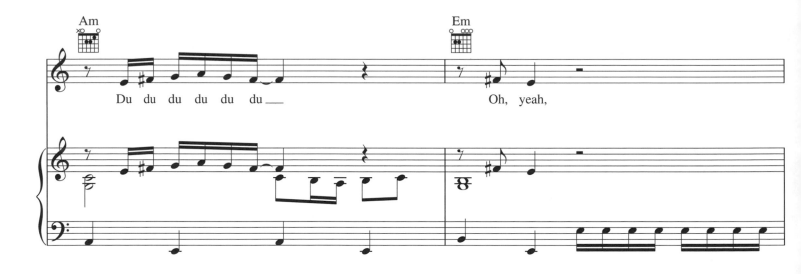

Du du du du du du _____ Oh, yeah,

She's well ac-quaint-ed with the touch of the vel-vet hand _____ like a liz-ard on a

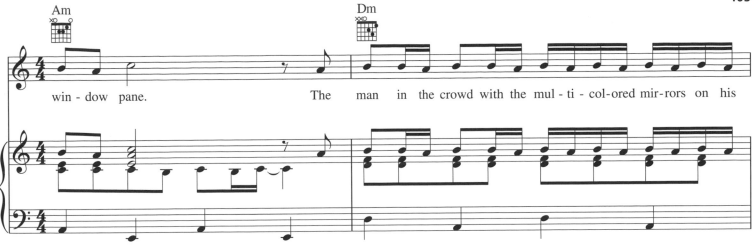

win- dow pane. The man in the crowd with the mul - ti - col-ored mir-rors on his

hob - nail boots, ly - ing with his eyes while his hands are bus — y work - ing

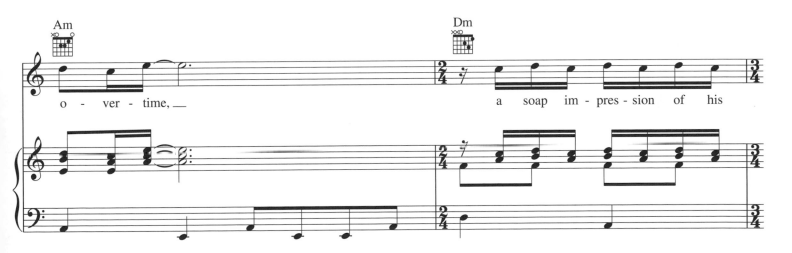

o - ver - time, __ a soap im - pres - sion of his

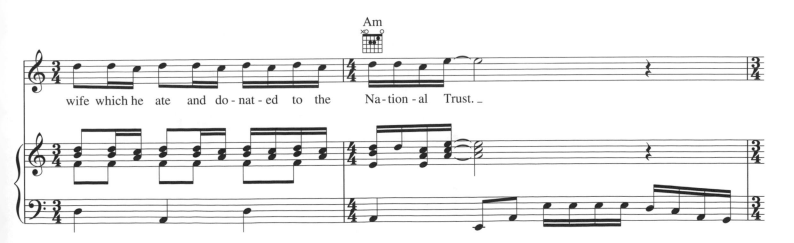

wife which he ate and do - nat - ed to the Na - tion - al Trust. __

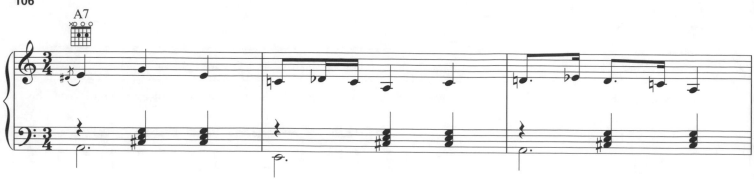

I need a fix 'cause I'm go - in' down, _____

down to the bits that I left up - town. ____

I need a fix 'cause I'm go - in' down. ____

Moth - er Su - per - i - or, jump the gun, ____

**Play 3 times**

Moth - er Su - per - i - or jump the gun. ____

# BLACKBIRD

Words and Music by JOHN LENNON
and PAUL McCARTNEY

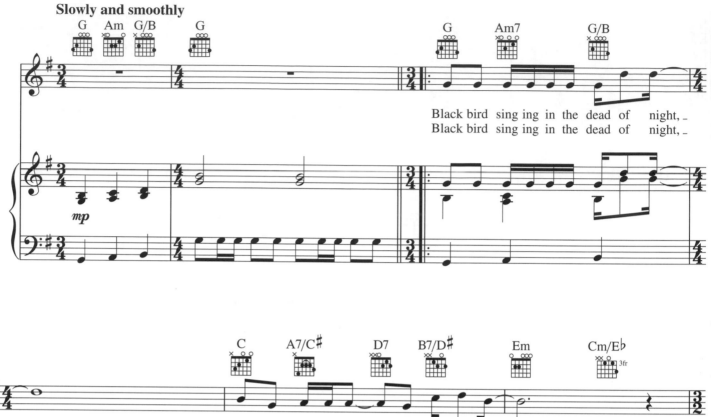

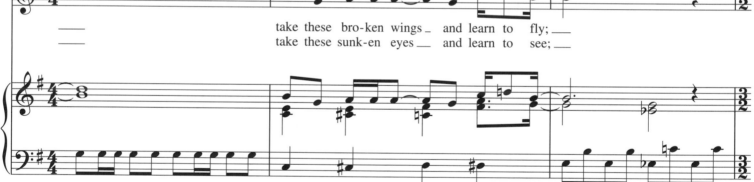

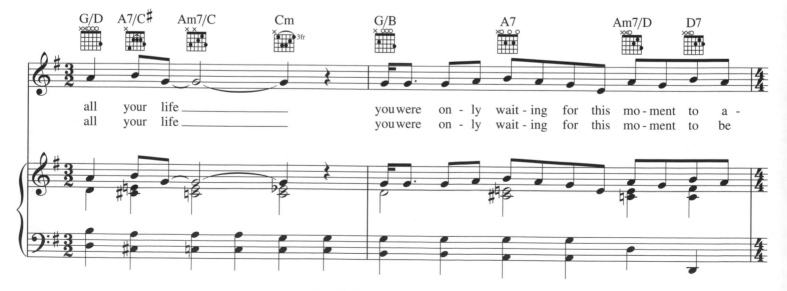

rise.            free.

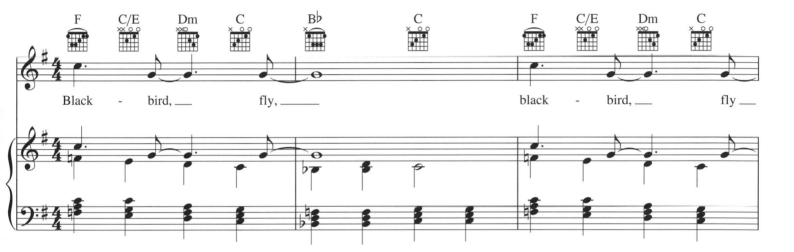

Black - bird, ___ fly, _____    black - bird, ___ fly ___

___   in - to the light of a dark black night. ____

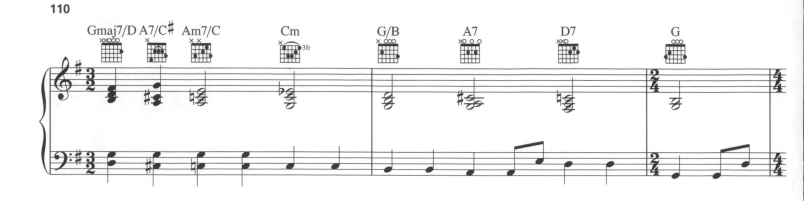

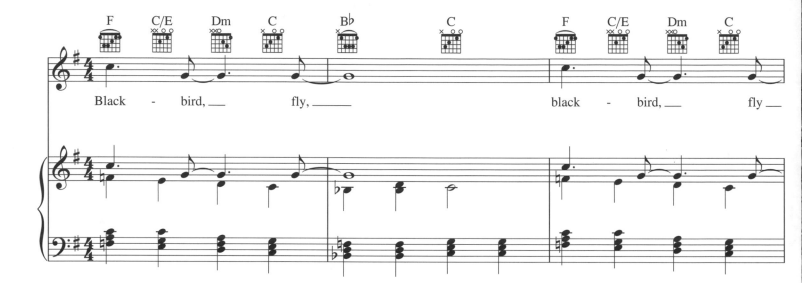

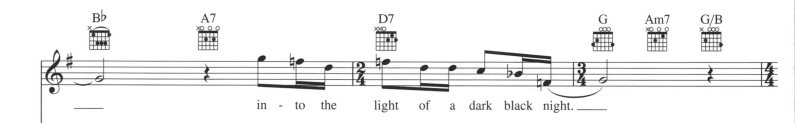

# HEY JUDE

Words and Music by JOHN LENNON
and PAUL McCARTNEY

Slowly

Hey Jude,_____ don't make it bad; take a
don't make it bad; take a

sad song_____ and make it bet - ter._____ Re-
sad song_____ and make it bet - ter._____ Re -

mem - ber to let her in - to your heart; then you can start___
mem - ber to let her un - der your skin, then you be - gin___

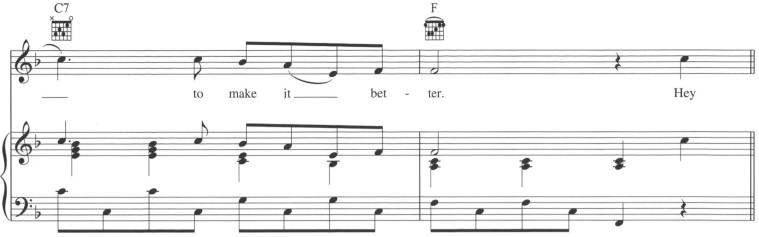

to make it ___ bet - ter.                                    Hey

Jude, _____ don't be a - fraid.          You were made to ___ go out and
Jude, _____ don't let me down.          You have found her, ___ now go and

get her. ___                                    The min - ute      you let her un - der your
get her. ___                                    Re - mem-ber      to let her in - to your

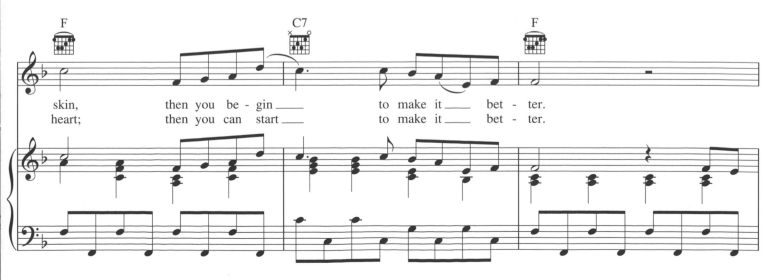

skin,          then you be - gin ___          to make it ___ bet - ter.
heart;         then you can start ___          to make it ___ bet - ter.

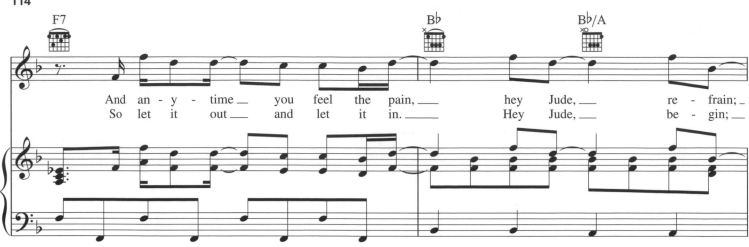

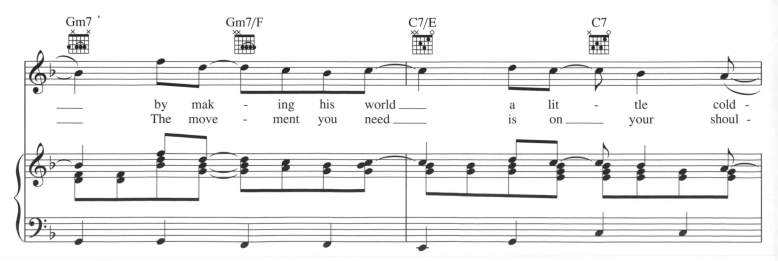

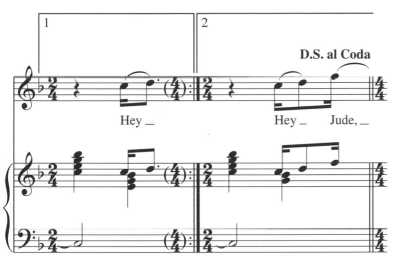

# DON'T LET ME DOWN

Words and Music by JOHN LENNON
and PAUL McCARTNEY

Don't let me down,

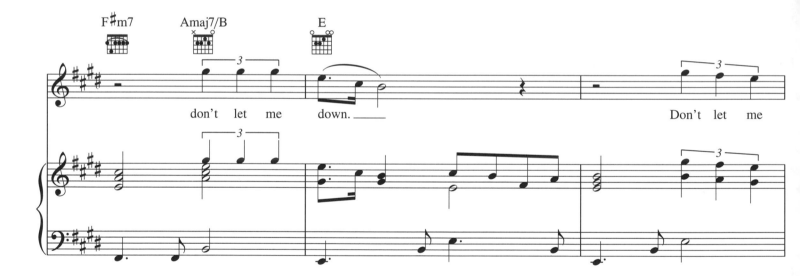

don't let me down. _____ Don't let me

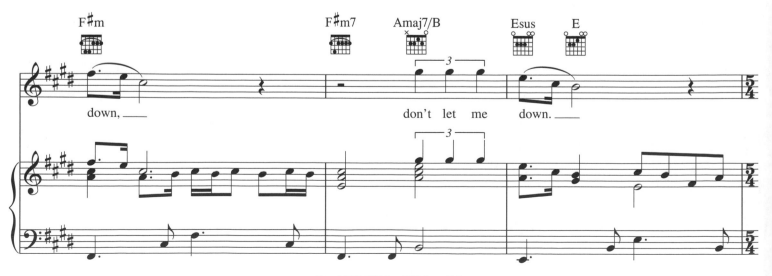

down, _____ don't let me down. _____

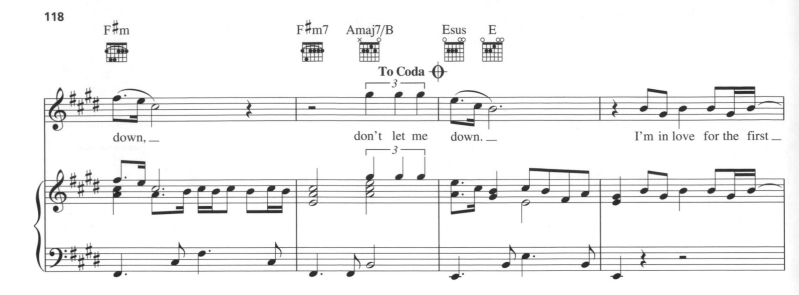

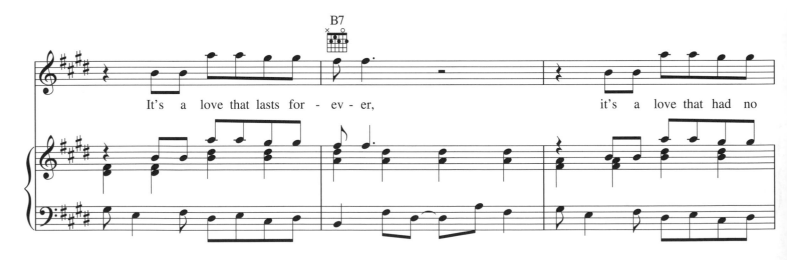

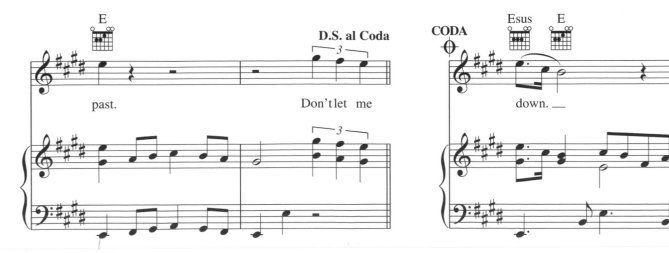

# ALL YOU NEED IS LOVE

Words and Music by JOHN LENNON
and PAUL McCARTNEY

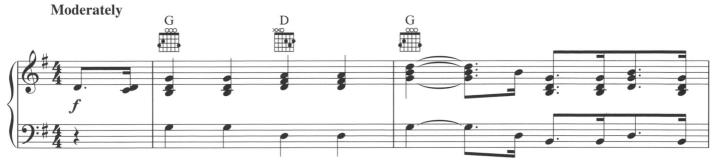

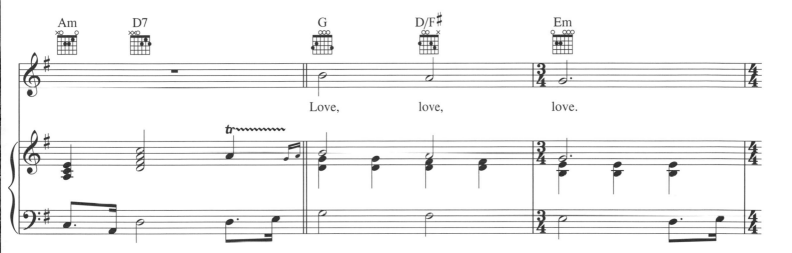

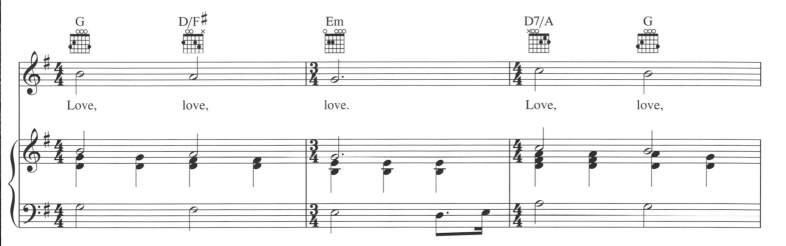

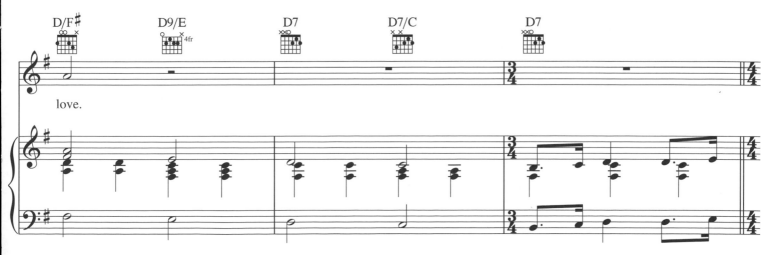

There's noth-ing you can do that can't be done. _____
There's noth-ing you can make that can't be made. _____
There's noth-ing you can know that is-n't known. _____

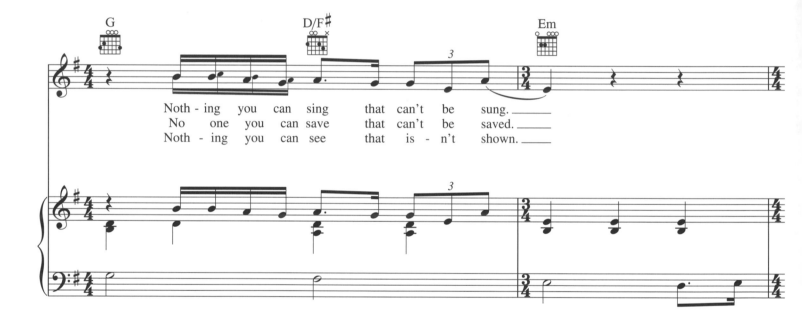

Noth-ing you can sing that can't be sung. _____
No one you can save that can't be saved. _____
Noth-ing you can see that is-n't shown. _____

Noth-ing you can say but you can learn _____ how to play the game. _____
Noth-ing you can do but you can learn _____ how to be you in time. _____ } It's
No-where you can be that is-n't where _____ you're meant to be. _____

eas - y.    All you need is love, ___

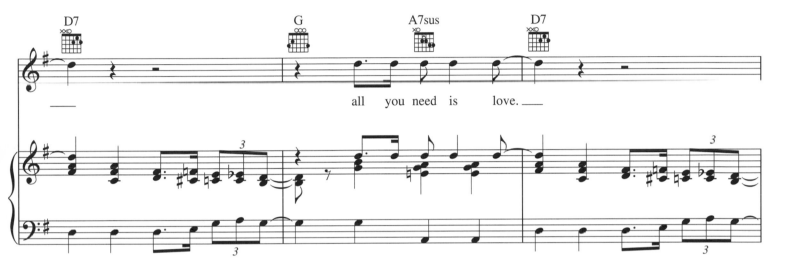

___    all you need is love. ___

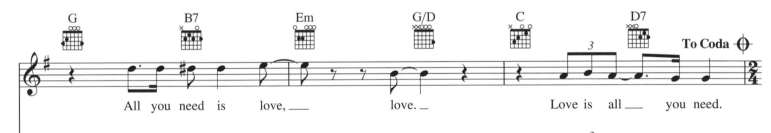

All you need is love, ___    love. ___    Love is all ___ you need.

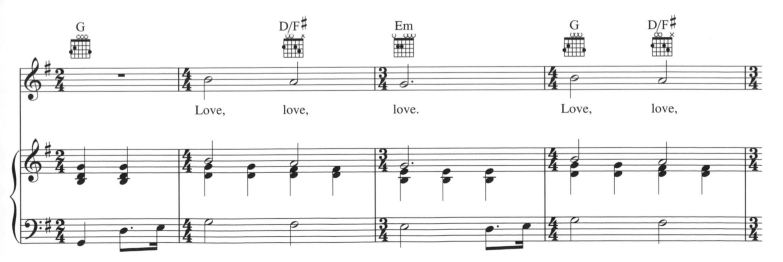

Love,    love,    love.    Love,    love,

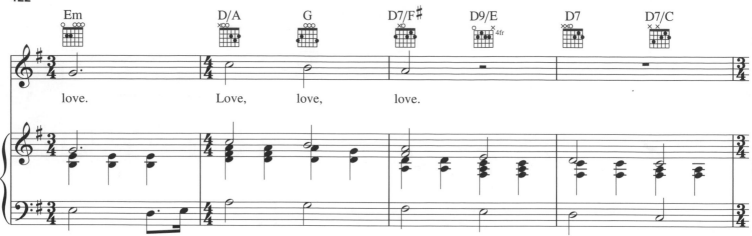

love. Love, love, love.

All you need is love, ___

all you need is love. ___ All you need is love, _

___ love. ___ Love is all ___ you need.

**D.S. al Coda**

# LUCY IN THE SKY WITH DIAMONDS

Words and Music by JOHN LENNON
and PAUL McCARTNEY

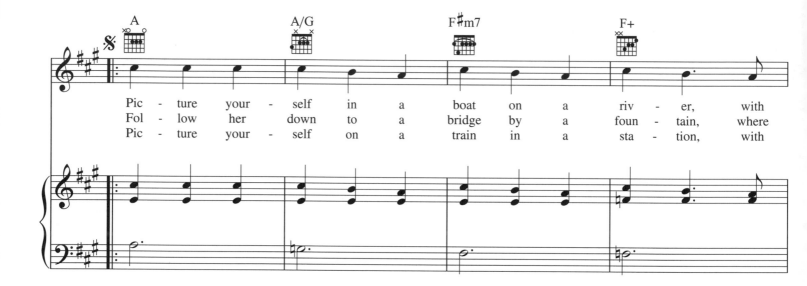

Pic - ture your - self in a boat on a riv - er, with
Fol - low her down to a bridge by a foun - tain, where
Pic - ture your - self on a train in a sta - tion, with

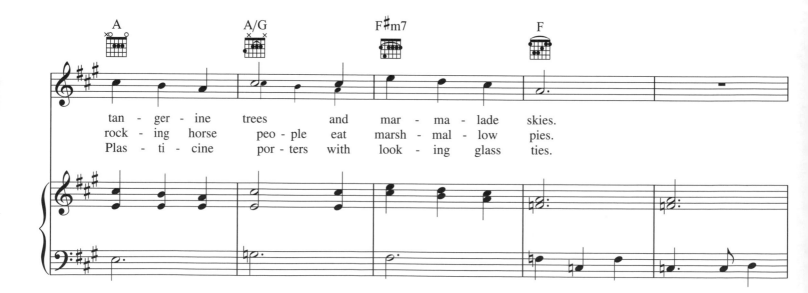

tan - ger - ine trees and mar - ma - lade skies.
rock - ing horse peo - ple eat marsh - mal - low pies.
Plas - ti - cine por - ters with look - ing glass ties.

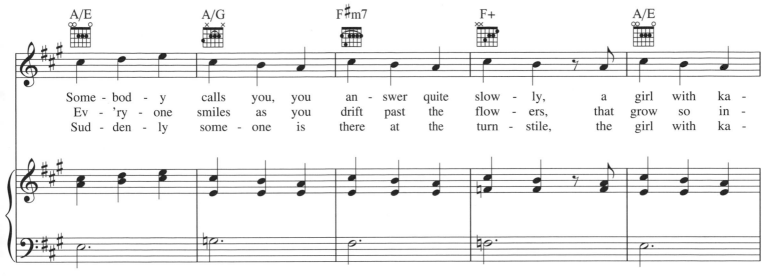

Somebody calls you, you answer quite slowly, a girl with ka-
Ev - 'ry - one smiles as you drift past the flow - ers, that grow so in -
Sud - den - ly some - one is there at the turn - stile, the girl with ka -

**To Coda** ⊕

lei - do - scope eyes. _____
cred - i - bly high. _____
lei - do - scope

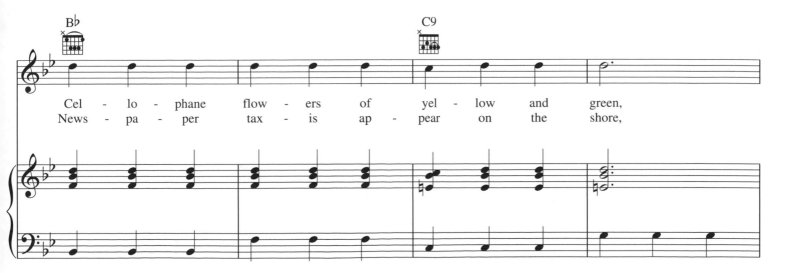

Cel - lo - phane flow - ers of yel - low and green,
News - pa - per tax - is ap - pear on the shore,

tow - er - ing o - ver your head. _____ Look for the
wait - ing to take you a - way. _____ Climb in the

girl with the sun in her eyes, and she's gone. }
back with your head in the clouds, and you're gone. }

Lu - cy in the sky ___ with dia - monds, Lu - cy in the sky ___ with

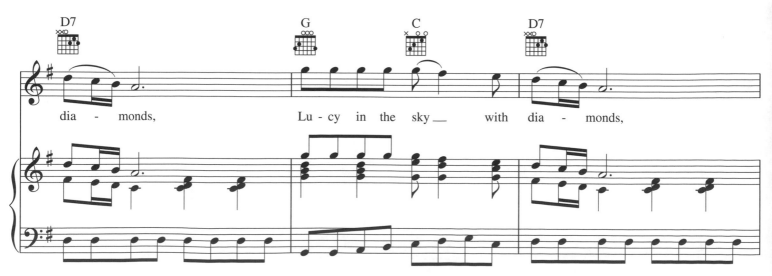

dia - monds, Lu - cy in the sky ___ with dia - monds,